Hilmar von Campe has led a lie of salvation from sin. The reader wi ated by von Campe's eloquent acco was complicit in evil to a man who r par excellence.

HOWARD PHILLIPS—two-time presidential candidate;
chairman of the Conservative Caucus

Thrilling and quite moving! I am touched and impressed by Hilmar von Campe's book *Defeating the Totalitarian Lie*. It reads extremely well, raises deep human and supernatural questions, comes from the heart, is very honest, and shows a real problem that we have in this world today: godlessness. It also shows how human beings are changed in their characters when they convert to the Christian faith. And immensely touching is the letter about the suffering of von Campe's father. What a pain but also what a consolation must it have been for von Campe's mom and children to know about his last days, full of terrible suffering but also full of love for his family. I learned a lot about the Second World War: the sufferings of the expellees from their homeland, the true nature of Hitler and Nazism, the cruelty of the Russians, and the falsity of the Allies. I am glad that I read this book! I am convinced that it will find many interested readers in this country, as it enables one to learn in a more differentiated way about German history, without propaganda. As the author says, I hope that that kind of history is not already on the way again…

MAIKE HICKSON—German after-war generation; Ph.D. and author

I was tremendously impressed with the main theme of the story, and, of course, I openly cried as I read about the suffering von Campe's dad had to endure. Also, I as a practicing Catholic applaud the author for his emphasis on the importance of keeping God's Commandments. I marvel at his insightfulness in targeting the ACLU as a destructive organization and appreciate his warning that we had better sit up and take notice.

ALBERT CHESTONE—FBI agent (ret.)

Hilmar von Campe's story is one of extravagant grace. Raised by God-fearing Christian parents in Germany and motivated like many of his generation by the cause of German Nationalism, von Campe served as a soldier in the German army during World War II. In the devastating aftermath of Germany's defeat and as the realities of Hitler's atrocities became widespread, von Campe began a deep personal process of repentance and pursuit of God's truth, which has led him to invest his life to the mission of educating cultures about the dangerous power of deception.

Von Campe understands better than most that truth is the platform upon which God's people must stand. He stands today as a prophet to our own culture in America. His story is not only fascinating because of its historical context, but also it is highly relevant. As philosopher, essayist, novelist and poet George Santayana wrote, "Those who cannot remember the past are condemned to repeat it." Von Campe's passion is penetrating and at times disconcerting, but his message is authentic.

I have known very few people in my life who understand grace at the level that von Campe has experienced it. He has not only accepted responsibility for his own sins but also for the sins of his fatherland, reminding us all that to be truly forgiven for any sin, we must accept our propensity for all sin. Only then can we know the total freedom of forgiveness.

BILL KIERCE—lead pastor, Jubilee Shores United Methodist Church

Defeating the Totalitarian Lie is dynamite with explosive potential to shape the moral composition of America and awaken its atrophied national conscience. Hilmar von Campe's personal saga is intensely dramatic and deeply human, evoking a torrid melting pot of emotions and sparking countless morally rich ideas through his candor in sharing his failures, tragedies and triumphs. The transposing of the impact that a nation's morality and attitude toward God has upon its destiny with von Campe's inside story of Hitler's rise and fall as a German citizen, along with his insights into the shrouded portions of the War's history, is huge. *Defeating the Totalitarian Lie* is a very powerful way to communicate the truth and holds much promise.

RICK KERN—journalist

I was asked what I think of German author Hilmar von Campe: "Is he an ordinary man who has sought to do a little good? A rigorous intellectual? A fraud?" As von Campe was unknown to me, I had a look at him and his work and after a first cursory assessment I'd definitely say that he is NOT a fraud.

What impresses me specifically is that he doesn't pose as a former rabid Nazi who saw the light but rather he stresses the fact that it was the looking the other way of ordinary people like himself that made the Nazi atrocities possible. I appreciate, too, that he seems to see the Communist crimes in perspective and doesn't reckon them up against the Nazi crimes, something only too many Germans like to do.

I appreciate, too, that he draws the inevitable parallels between Nazi Germany and the recent Muslim threat. It requires a lot of courage to do that.

Hilmar von Campe's biography bears witness to the fact that the secular, leftist/liberal ideologies are no answer to the totalitarian and inhuman threats now, as they weren't an answer then.

NORA BRINKER—independent German journalist
and translator with an MA in history;
a former socialist and agnostic who found a faith in God

It is my pleasure to recommend Hilmar von Campe to the Body of Christ. Hilmar has in my opinion an international perspective that touches deeply on where we are in America today… Hilmar also speaks a message of reconciliation that is so vital to the work of the Kingdom of God today.

PASTOR JEFF KIPP—Shoesh David, The Root of David Messianic

Experience with lies led this man to teach the value of truth. Von Campe has spent his life traveling around the world meeting people and promoting the belief that freedom can only exist if based on truth.

BRENDA G. ANDERSON—*Press-Register,* Mobile, Alabama

DEFEATING THE TOTALITARIAN LIE

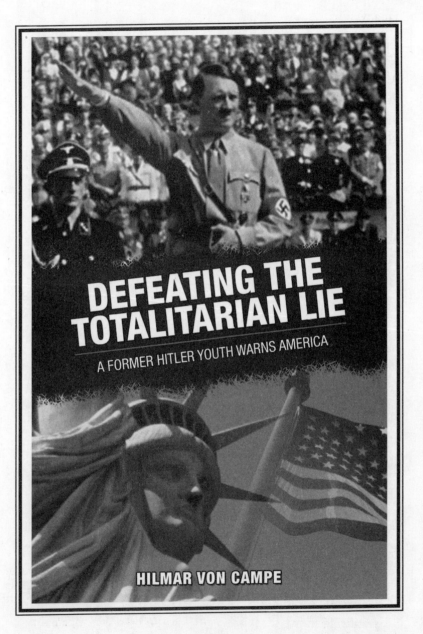

DEFEATING THE TOTALITARIAN LIE

A FORMER HITLER YOUTH WARNS AMERICA

HILMAR VON CAMPE

HighWay

A division of Anomalos Publishing House

Crane

HighWay

A division of Anomalos Publishing House, Crane 65633

© 2008 by Hilmar von Campe

Printed in the United States of America

09   3

ISBN -10: 0981509193 (paper)

EAN-13: 9780981509198 (paper)

Cover illustration and design by Steve Warner

A CIP catalog record for this book is available from the Library of Congress.

CONTENTS

Foreword xiii

Preface xv

Acknowledgments xvii

Introduction 1

Chapter 1: From the Jaws of Death 5
    As Prisoner of War
    The Escape Begins
    Crossing Enemy Territory
    Destiny Touches Me

Chapter 2: Nazi Power 19
    How Was It Possible?
    The Character of Hitler
    The Nazis Fire My Father
    The Consequences of World War I
    Our Family Life in Nazi Germany
    The Persecution of the Jews
    The Road to a Totalitarian Society

Chapter 3: Beginning of World War II 49
    The Official Version
    What Really Happened

Chapter 4: The War 53
    My Brother Fell
    The Soviet Union Enters the War
    Godlessness and Self Destruction
    My Military Service
    Resistance to Hitler
    Hans and Sophie Scholl, Dietrich Bonhoeffer
    The July 20, 1944, Coup d'Etat

Chapter 5: The Bombing..71

Chapter 6: The End of the War..75
The Suffering of My Father
The Fate of 3.5 million Sudeten-Germans
The Red Army Rapes, Loots, Kills, and Burns Down Whole
*   Villages in the East German Provinces*

Chapter 7: The Years after the War...93
As Refugees in the West
Clash with the British Army
The Cucumber Stealing
The Power of Hatred
Our Landlords
The Nazi Issue Haunts Us
Hamburg University
The Winds of Change
Listen to God
Who Runs the Nation?
A New Family
Restitution

Chapter 8: The Next Thirty Years 123

Chapter 9: Mexican Experiences 127
The Godless Government Establishment
My Workforce
The Thief Who Was My Partner
My Prime Client
My Family
Resume

Chapter 10: The Real Neo-Nazis...139
      Definition of a Neo-Nazi
      The Lack of Understanding Ideology
      The Soviet Strategy
      The Chinese Unrestricted Warfare
      The Quranic Concept of War
      The PLO, Hamas, Hezbollah and Others
      Soviet Involvement

Chapter 11: The State of Israel...169

Chapter 12: The Encirclement of America.................................179

Chapter 13: Robert Mugabe, the Disgrace of Zimbabwe.........185

Chapter 14: The Enemy Within...189

Chapter 15: No to the North American Union Collective.........203

Chapter 16: The United Nations Hoax.....................................207

Chapter 17: Systems of Lies...213

Chapter 18: The Role of God in Human Society......................217
      The Dictatorship of Relativism
      The Confusion of Christians
      The Lost Purpose of History
      Revolution of Truth and Freedom

Appendix A: The National Institute for Truth and Freedom
           Objectives..231

Appendix B: The International Biographical Center
in Cambridge, England 233

Appendix C: The Weizmann-Faisal Agreement 235

Bibliography 239

About the Author 241

FOREWORD

THIS IS THE second edition of my book *How Was It Possible?*, which was published in October 2006. Since then a growing number of political developments have emerged which threaten American sovereignty. We also face financial disaster while chaos in our society grows. Like in Germany before Hitler, a great part of our population doesn't know any more the difference between right and wrong and elect the wrong people into office who apply the Marxist and not the American way in their policies. The two philosophies are incompatible. Every day brings this nation closer to a Nazi-style totalitarian abyss. Mainly because of the relevance of it to my writing I decided to produce this second edition with a new title to define our enemies within and outside better, describe what they have in common and point out what to do about it.

I lived the Nazi nightmare, and as the old saying goes, "A man with an experience is never at the mercy of a man with an argument." Everything I write is based on my personal experience in Nazi Germany. There is nothing theoretical about my description of what happens when a nation throws God out of government and society, and Christians become religious bystanders. I don't want to see a repetition. The role of God in human society is the decisive issue for this generation. My writing is part of my life of restitution for the crimes of a godless government, of the evil of which I was a part.

My restitution includes a commitment to the state of Israel and the God-given rights of the Jewish people.

PREFACE

WHENEVER SOMEBODY ANYWHERE in the world wants to describe an evil person such as Saddam Hussein or an evil cause such as the Nazi philosophy, he or she refers to Adolf Hitler. Along with Hitler and Saddam Hussein, the President of Iran, Mahmoud Ahmadinejad would meet the criteria of an evil person as well. Yet, most of those who refer to Hitler have very little idea what it was really like in Nazi Germany. Nor do they understand how it was possible for a group of criminals to deceive an entire nation about their true nature and commit the atrocities for which the Holocaust is representative.

The consummate spin master, Mahmoud Ahmadinejad, is just as much a liar as Adolf Hitler was. When he denies the existence of the Holocaust and promotes the elimination of Israel, he only demonstrates his ignorance and lack of moral integrity, which puts him in the same unprincipled company of the Nazi dictator. Can a Moslem be close to Hitler and to true religion at the same time? Is any Christian who professes his faith in God with words but acts with the same indifference to others as the Nazis really a Christian? I deal with this issue in my book.

I grew up under the Nazis, was in the Hitler Youth and fought against the Red Army in the Yugoslavian theater as a tank gunner (assault artillery) in the German Army. I was captured at the end of the war and five months later escaped from a prisoner of war camp in Communist Yugoslavia. My family was crushed by Nazis and Soviets and paid dearly for 12 years of Nazi rule.

It took me a long time to understand and define the nature of National Socialism, an extreme leftwing branch of the global Socialist movement, because Nazis are not Fascists as many believe, they are radical left wing Socialists. And unfortunately, their philosophy continues to flourish under different labels remaining a menace to America and free human society.

The most painful part of defining National Socialism was to recognize my own moral responsibility for the Nazi disaster and their crimes against humanity. It boiled down to the accepting the truth that "as I am, so is my nation," and realizing that if every German was like me, it was no wonder that the nation became a cesspool of gangsters. This realization is as valid today for any person in any nation as it was then, and it is true for America and every American now.

At a breakfast of the Retired Officers' Association in Colorado Springs in 1995, I thanked those veterans present for having defeated Hitler which enabled me to live in freedom and not in a Nazi society. German voters have since installed a democratic government and parliament, thankfully establishing political freedom.

Since then, however, I have realized that political freedom and democratic rules alone are not sufficient to govern humanity. Democratic procedures can be subverted and dishonest politicians are like sand in the gearbox, abundant, everywhere, and destructive. What I see in America today is people painting their cabins while the ship goes down.

Today in America we are witnessing a repeat performance of the tragedy of 1933 when an entire nation let itself be led like a lamb to the Socialist slaughterhouse. This time, the end of freedom is inevitable unless America rises to her mission and destiny.

ACKNOWLEDGMENTS

I AM GRATEFUL to my wife and my children, Stefan, Sabrina and her husband Marcelo Lew, and my sister Sibylle, who participated in the development of the theme of this book all along and commented on what I wrote. Stefan had suggested many times that I should write a biography. I am indebted to Howard Phillips who suggested and encouraged me to write this book, to his son Douglas whose video-interview of me in his home provided the basis for the story and to Tom Horn and his team who have brought this book into the market.

I owe special gratitude to Dr. James Dobson, Paul Batura and Focus on the Family who supported me. A warm thank you goes to John Andrews, Chuck Baynard, Alfred Chestone, John Hargreaves, Sharon Hughes, Rick Kern, Denise Lindross, Dr. Paul Muenstermann, Craig Nickisch for helping me in various aspects of putting this story together.

INTRODUCTION

THIS BOOK IS an expression of my concern for America and Western culture. My intention is to awaken our slumbering nation to the dangers we are facing individually and collectively. Today, living in America as a U.S citizen, I am increasingly reminded of the manner in which the Nazis maneuvered and cheated us. When I watch developments in society and analyze the political process, I shudder—especially when I look at the reasoning behind foreign policy decisions.

Furthermore, listening to empty sermons in countless churches of different denominations, I recognize the spiritual parallels to the nightmares my family experienced living in Nazi Germany. The silence from our pulpits regarding the moral collapse of American society from within is not very different from the silence that echoed from the pulpits in Germany toward Nazi policies.

As objectively as possible, I describe critical historic essentials, many unknown to most people, that unfolded before, during, and after the 12 years of Nazi rule. I profile what their reign of terror meant to my family and me, and then relate these experiences, events, and their motivations to contemporary America and the rest of the world.

I want the reader to understand that as important as an individual event might be, the decisive factor is not the event itself. The decisive factor is the one thing you don't see—the motive—the "why" that led to the event. Very often the motives of someone, or some group, with a decisive influence on an event or development, are never mentioned in

1

the context of that event. I also explore patterns in these motives that can give you insight into a much bigger picture, and prepare you for coming events outside your world. I describe how "little me" can make a big difference.

My writing confronts this unseen substance and the purpose driving so many critical events and developments. Among the examples I mention are the ACLU and HAMAS. When I see how much of the legal community is forcing God out of society, I cannot help but remember the German Gestapo (Secret State Police) agents on Sunday mornings. They would gather in front of our church attempting to intimidate those of us who came to worship God by writing down our names in full view of everyone.

It was a fearful time as we all knew the consequences of falling out of grace with the Nazis. These Gestapo agents reinforced the same message I was given by the Nazis in the Hitler Youth and in school. With disdain they assured us we could pray and sing hymns at home or in church as much as we liked, but Christianity, they insisted, had no role to play in the rules of society. It was made clear, that structuring the culture was the exclusive business of the Nazi state, a mantle the ACLU seems to wear proudly—only they leave the word "Nazi" out.

Hamas, Hezbollah, and similar organizations are actually Marxist/Leninist in their thinking, only with a religious label. Their leaders and followers are ruthless and godless Socialists. Saddam Hussein's Baath Party was a Socialist party. "Islam is a political and social system as well as a religious faith" defines Robert Spencer. The same is true for Marxism/Leninism and National Socialism. What makes them different from Fascism is their purpose, ruthlessness and worldview. All materialistic ideologies are based on lies, as I shall illustrate. In this book, I will unveil the Ideology of Freedom which, unlike materialistic ideologies, is moral in nature and based on the truth of God.

The separation of two institutions, the church and the state, was promoted by the Nazis and cunningly driven by a lie. What they really pursued was the separation of God and His Commandments from the German people. The Nazis knew that a commitment to God and His absolute moral standards before government would be a great obstacle to exercising their power based on immorality and contempt for life and other people's rights. In the case of the ACLU, their target is the American people, and like the Nazis they lie about their reasons. They speak of defending the civil rights of Americans, but that is not true. Just as the Nazis did, they strive to cut the connection of the American people to God, Christian morality, history, and traditions. By doing so, they are cleverly preparing the moral ground in America to cultivate and harvest the Socialist/Atheist seed.

What they are propagating is not significantly different from the Nazi philosophy. When I point out that Nazi stands for National Socialist and the ACLU has a Communist/Socialist background, it demonstrates the ideological similarities in the two groups. "I am for socialism, disarmament, and ultimately for abolishing the state itself. I seek social ownership of property, the abolition of the propertied class and sole control by those who produce wealth. Communism is the goal," stated Roger Baldwin, the founder of the ACLU. The greater problem, however, is not so much what they do, but that they continue to get away with it. After all our Constitution is based on Christian teachings and there are 50 states in the Union that also base their Constitutions on God.

I am not trying to dole out blame but instead report facts and their consequences as objectively as I can. I recount my own experience for I have discovered that you can't build a firm future unless you face the past and put things right. Each individual and each nation begins change with their self and their nation as I have done, not with others as the Socialists/Liberals do.

Our family lived through the Nazi years in Germany, an experience typical of millions of Europeans regardless of what side they were on. We paid a high price for the moral perversions of a German government, which excluded God and His Commandments from their policies. America must not continue following the same path to destruction, but instead heed the lessons of history and the warning I am giving.

I am committed to the destiny and mission of the United States, which is to be a nation under God, with the purpose to make freedom available to all of humanity. There is no other nation in the world that can do it. In spite of the relentless assault on our values and sovereignty there is still more moral substance in the United States than anywhere else in the world. However, to accomplish this mission, profound personal and national change is necessary. Countering the attack on the family and the school systems is critical; it is too reminiscent of the moral incursion led by the Nazis.

I watched godlessness bring Germany down and I know from personal experience that God is the answer; any contrary arguments won't shake me. He alone can resurrect this abortion-ridden, promiscuous, and self-centered society with a corrupt government establishment as the light of morality fades from our hearts. At the writing of this book we are in the throes of countless immoral and anti-God forces across the globe, which are merging into a dark coalition. Their purpose is to eliminate God and a free society, and establish a totalitarian regime. Without the truth of God and a change in the motivation of human nature on a sweeping scale, lasting freedom will not be possible.

CHAPTER ONE

FROM THE JAWS OF DEATH

As Prisoner of War

MAY 8, 1945, found Germany unconditionally surrendering to the Allied forces. It also found my unit, a battery of the Assault Artillery Brigade 191, entrenched in a reserve position in Yugoslavia. I don't remember the name of the river that wound its way ribbon-like through the valley, but I do recall it was in the Southern part of Slovenia. Knowing that the war was lost, we all had the same distant look in our eyes even though the full force of its reality had not yet slammed into us.

The ceasefire agreement between the Soviet and German forces in the Yugoslavian theatre was not yet in force as far as we knew, it was still open season on Germans. Nevertheless, the enemy seemed miles away and we felt safe enough to don our swimming trunks and relax in a garden near the river. Our tanks and vehicles were parked outside the abandoned house next to the garden as our gazes wandered through the azure skies and basked in the warmth of the sun.

With no idea what the future would hold for us, we decided to make the most of every moment. "Peace will be dreadful," we rightfully thought demoralized by the prospect of enemy occupation. The intoxicating fragrance of chicken and potatoes roasting in the oven for lunch swirled through the house bringing back memories of better days.

Suddenly all hell broke loose as machine gun fire from the nearby hills strafed the house and yard. It was sheer panic as everyone jumped to their feet, grabbed their clothes and scrambled for cover.

As foolish as it may seem I did not want our chickens to be eaten by Soviet soldiers or Yugoslavian partisans, so I asked my crew to wait a minute while I rushed to the kitchen. Bullets kicked up dust at my heels as I threw open the oven doors only to discover that the succulent poultry and potatoes were gone! Another burst of machine gun fire made it clear that there was no time to search for our lunch.

Fuming, I joined the others and off we drove, grateful that we had no casualties but seething that we had no chickens. Frustrated, I pondered the fate of the missing foul and I finally realized that I had simply overlooked a door on the other side of the stove. Needless to say I was not a happy camper.

In the coming months when we were close to starvation, most of the time my hunger was relentless causing me to dream of those lost chickens and fantasize that I was a messenger for a bakery where I could eat as many rolls as I desired.

Soon after this we were apprised of the conditions of our surrender and discovered that we were required to deliver our tanks and weapons to the victors, but permitted to keep our vehicles so we could return to Austria in them. After a long discussion we finally decided to abide by the conditions of the surrender, left our tanks on the roadside, and drove in direction of the border. Sadly, it didn't take long to learn that our dream of going home was to remain just that: a dream.

We entered what appeared to be a deserted village and carefully made our way to the market place located in its center. Suddenly we were surrounded by partisans shooting in the air, screaming as they dragged us from our vehicles at gunpoint. The partisans were the Communist fighters of the Tito forces whom I had never met in combat, but who were obviously our captors now. The Soviet High Command had broken the terms of the surrender, which should have been anticipated. The German High Command had been naïve and should have negotiated the right for its soldiers to keep their arms until they arrived safely at the border.

That marked the beginning of two weeks of living hell we called the "Death March." Two hundred thousand German soldiers were moved into camps, marching in tidy little columns with no food. We watched in mute horror the bodies on the side of the road as Croatians and Germans were killed but we were forced to continue on with no idea what awaited us. By the time evening came, the pain and fatigue made it impossible to stand on our feet any longer. Many of us just collapsed and crawled to the only sanctuary we could find: sleep. Each day brought the same savage ordeal.

Early on we had discussed the option of leaving the column of prisoners and escaping to Austria. It would have been easy to disappear into the woods, but we abandoned the idea, realizing that we would have had to cross the Alps, a trial we were not prepared for. As the days dragged on and I grew weaker, for the first time since I entered combat I considered the possibility that I might not survive this nightmare.

After about two weeks, the march ended at a camp where we remained for several weeks. Food was scarce and consisted of corn bread, completely rotten inside, and black bean soup, which was hot water with some beans in it. Then, a number of us were dispatched to a work camp in the middle of a forest where we had to cut trees.

We were forbidden to leave the camp, located close to a river, under punishment of death. Risking the death penalty, I cautiously went down to the river nearly every night and each time I was able to pick up a good quantity of mussels. As time went by, I expanded my nightly excursions with some others to fields further away, where we unearthed potatoes in their early stages. Thankfully we were moved to another camp before the peasants noticed what had happened. I was still alive.

The new camp was a weathered old barn in a small mountain village, where many houses had been destroyed during the war. We had one lonely guard that longed for his girlfriend who lived in a neighboring village. Time crawled on agonizingly, and by October the days and nights grew so cold and food was so scarce that it forced us to continue our nightly excursions into the surrounding potato fields. At some point I reluctantly came to the conclusion that I would not survive the winter. The lack of food and clothing assured our demise and as if that was not enough, the population's hatred against anything German sealed our fate—they would never help us. I was not alone in my gloomy realization; four of my comrades came to the same conclusion. At first it brought a sense of resignation and peace but surprisingly that turned into an angry resolve prompting us to act.

THE ESCAPE BEGINS

At ten o'clock in the night of October 10, 1945, when our guard was visiting his girlfriend, five of us defied the Communist partisans and set out to reach home. With one map, we had to walk northeast to reach Hungary by crossing the river Drau, and continue north to Austria. Once inside their borders, we could cross the demarcation line between the Soviet and British occupation armies. That was the decisive boundary between slavery and death in Siberia, or freedom with its boundless hope.

We walked in a line with about 100 yards between each other. I was in second place behind a police officer who had the map. After having walked for about two hours, we reached a quiet village and thought everyone was asleep. All of a sudden the stillness was broken by shouting as the sharp crackling of gunfire lit the night. Apparently our police officer had run into a Partisan patrol.

Instinctively I bolted left and fled as fast as I could into the cover of the nearby fields. The other three did the same without anyone giving a command or seeing each other. By pure miracle we all met again in the heart of the night in a random field a safe distance from the patrol. Without pause we continued walking and though we no longer had a map, we knew the direction. The cloudless sky boasted a brilliant tapestry of shimmering stars allowing the North Star to guide us every night. To this day, I don't know what happened to our lead man but fear the worst.

When daylight approached we took cover in a forest or sought shelter in whatever hiding place we could find. We ate anything we could find including raw turnips, a delicacy which we dug out of the fields we passed. One morning the only thing we found for hiding were some bushes on the side of a of lonely country road. We had no choice so we dove into them.

A few hours later a man came along with his dog on the leash walking his dog. The dog strained at his leash as it smelled us, barked, and pulled his master to the bushes. I looked straight into the faces of the man and his four-legged companion while he did the same, sizing me up as we stared at each other. Fear crawled up my spine like a venomous serpent only to slither off as the strange duo grunted and quietly went on their way. We spent the rest of the blessedly uneventful day very uncomfortable hiding out in a prickly thicket of bushes.

After trudging about ten days we found ourselves stopped on the banks of a rushing river. The moon was nearly full and by this time the nights were dreadfully bitter. I told myself that I would not swim through the frigid water to reach the other side, and decided instead to risk my life, take my chances, and surrender.

We finally made our way to the river's edge only to discover a boat resting against its bank underwater. Our spirits buoyed, we had one sailor in our ranks who organized us, and got the craft seaworthy. Hesitantly we rowed across the vast stream expecting to be shot at by border guards because we thought the river marked the border to Hungary. Nothing happened! Nobody shot at us. Without incident we started walking again and eventually noticed slogans painted on the walls of houses that told us we were still in Yugoslavia. Our spirits sank as we realized we had only crossed one arm of the river.

During the second night we reached the main arm of the river and amazingly there was another boat tied to a tree at the very spot we approached the river. We were able to cross the river without any incident, crossing the border into Hungary. Jubilation! We had left the enemy territory with the Tito partisans behind us. Unfortunately, we were not out of the woods for Hungary was occupied by the Red Army. However, unlike Yugoslavia the Hungarian people were hospitable and friendly going out of their way to help us and that turned out to be the difference between life and death.

CROSSING ENEMY TERRITORY

At daybreak we ventured over to a weathered farmhouse and cautiously knocked at the door. When the occupants answered we explained who we were, what we had in mind, and asked for their help. Compassion shined from their eyes as they immediately invited us into their home and gave us food. Thanks to their graciousness we ate a real meal for the first time in months and were treated to a restful night's sleep in the barn. When night fell again, we went on our way and continued walking. We realized, however, that four hungry men would be too great a burden for one farmer so we split up into pairs and went to different houses.

On one occasion, we had not found a house yet though the sun had already risen. When we finally did discover a small farmhouse there were only two women living in it. Tragically, such living arrangements were not unusual at that time due to war casualties and the countless men who were taken prisoner by the Soviets when Hungary surrendered. The two women fed us and then we settled down to sleep in the barn to rest before continuing our journey. But before we even fell asleep, our two hostesses came rushing into the barn screaming that Soviet soldiers were coming for us. We jumped to our feet and ran outside to see a group of soldiers striding swiftly in our direction with a German shepherd straining against its leash. Their random shooting into the air, told us they meant business. Someone must have seen us entering the farmhouse and alerted the Soviets.

With our few belongings at hand, we scurried through a freshly plowed field towards a grove of nearby trees. The footsteps we left behind were clearly visible and to make matters worse, during all the commotion I had left my cap back in the farm. As if to assure my capture, all my papers, including my army identification booklet, had fallen from my uniform jacket and were scattered across the field in front of the trees we were hiding in. The booklet I had dropped was a wealth of personal information documenting locations where I had served, promotions, and decorations. There was no way to return and pick them up because the Soviet patrol had reached the farm at the same time we disappeared into the thicket.

I peered anxiously through the rustling leaves at the deadly documents that fluttered like stark white flags in the breeze against the rich brown field. "This is the end of our escape," I thought, mustering all the courage I could to face what was coming.

We watched preoccupied as the soldiers searched the farm. They picked up my cap and continued shooting into the air. The dog kept barking pulling so hard at its leash that I thought it would snap any second. Then, inexplicably they wandered off in the opposite direction and never came back. We stood there staring at each other in stunned disbelief for all they had to do was follow our footprints. At the time there seemed to be no plausible explanation as to why they didn't track us, but I will come to that a little later on.

As the sun slipped behind the jagged horizon we returned to the farmhouse to find our two hostesses trembling with fear. We all knew they faced certain execution should the Soviets catch them with us in the house, as would we. I am ashamed to say that I was so absorbed by my own plight that I completely disregarded the danger we put them in and instead sat comfortably in their easy chair asking for more food. Hands shaking, they served us what they had. Only after we were well fed did we leave. In retrospect I can see that I was seething with pride, arrogantly touting what I conceived to be my superlative organizational skills.

With our narrow escape being far too close for comfort, we decided to trade our uniforms for civilian clothes which were donated by our next hosts. We pressed on toward Austria but before entering any village, we asked the locals if there were any Soviet soldiers around. On one occasion we were told the coast was clear so we entered only to discover that the center of the town was swarming with enemy soldiers. I felt the color drain from my face as a Soviet officer and Hungarian policeman advanced directly toward us from the other side of the market place. Again my heart sank, and automatically, I put one foot in front of the other bracing myself for the worst. But the two men scarcely looked at us as they breezed by and disappeared into a nearby bar. Shaken, we left the village as quickly as possible.

Once we were at a safe distance away, my friend Tuennes and I had a candid discussion about how to approach villages in the future. Tuennes was the same age as I, and normally a cheerful Rhinelander from Duesseldorf. Visibly disturbed, he insisted he would never set foot in a village again but walk around it. Sparks flew as I argued it would take too long and carefully entering the village right away instead was well worth the risk because it was more important to reach safe haven as soon as possible. Neither of us could convince the other, so we went our separate ways.

We had memorized the address of a farm in Austria belonging to friends of the police officer whom we had lost at the beginning of our escape and agreed to meet there should we become separated at any point. So bidding each other farewell, we split up hoping to rendezvous at the farmhouse as free men.

My journey continued with no more incidents and eventually I reached a quaint little Hungarian town nestled off the beaten path on the Austrian border. I knocked on what seemed to be a friendly door and a very compassionate family took me in and gave me excellent food and a real bed. The next morning, my host led me deep into a forest chatting cordially. He slowly stopped, turned to me, and explained that I was now in Austria and should be very careful crossing the border near Graz which was occupied by British forces.

That evening, I arrived at a village close to the border. A mere mile away from freedom the countless dreams of this moment swept across me like warm summer breezes in the frigid chill. I had eaten, slept, and breathed thoughts of getting this far but never really expected it to happen. A kindly farmer put me up for the night and alerted me that I had but to cross a small bridge very early the next morning before the guard arrived at sunrise. "It is very easy," he said, assuring me that I should sleep in peace and I could trust him to wake me in time. Confident in his integrity, I retired to sleep in the stable.

I awoke with a start to the sunlight pouring through the windows like syrup; the farmer had forgotten to awaken me. Morning had barely broken but I just didn't have the poise or presence of mind to endure another twenty-four hours until I was out of danger and free. Instead, I took off at a run to try to reach the bridge before the guard took is post. As soon as I left the village, I saw the bridge in the distance and to my relief there was no Soviet soldier to be seen. Flanked on the left by a solitary farm, the bridge rested against the backdrop of a picturesque patch of woods, a winding trail leading to a narrow path beyond. I quickly walked toward it.

As I drew within 300 feet of the farm, a Soviet soldier suddenly appeared decisively striding toward me. Though his rifle remained slung over his shoulder, my blood seemed to freeze in my veins. I continued on mechanically; hope draining from my broken heart. This time I really saw no chance, having struggled all this way I found myself at the threshold of freedom only to find myself staring down the barrel of a gun.

Beads of sweat gathered on my brow as I thought that, after all this time, freedom was going to be taken from me. All had been for nothing. I hung my head and put one foot in front of the other. Just then, the path split, and a small lane veered left to the farm. Without much thought I followed it up to the door of the house. Having arrived, I knocked, or rather pretended to knock, since I had no intention of bringing out the occupants whose loyalties were unknown to me. Standing there with my back turned toward the Soviet soldier, I expected a great mass to approach from behind and grab me by the neck. Still I was determined to go out with my dignity intact so I pulled up my shoulders, drew myself to my full height, and waited for the inevitable.

Nothing happened! Finally, I gathered my courage and looked around carefully. The soldier had walked on and was already nearing the village. I was on the other side of the bridge in no time.

DESTINY TOUCHES ME

Perhaps it really is true that you don't know what you got until you lose it and it is only a person who has lost his or her freedom can truly appreciate it. Crossing that bridge was a defining moment that wrenched my life from the death grip the Soviets had on it and delivered it back into my own hands. Everybody in Germany knew what to expect from the Soviets: nothing good, but now I had broken away from their cruelty and was free.

On the other hand, we knew that the Western powers were our road to freedom. As I lay on a hill in Austria overlooking a village full of British soldiers, it sank into me that I had achieved what I set out to do. My mind went back to the many narrow escapes and events that could only be described as miracles, such as the boats in not one but two rivers, or the Soviet patrol with the dog apparently struck with blindness. Then it occurred to me that it could have been God who had led me out of bondage and cleared my way of obstacles. The next thought followed immediately, suggesting that if it had really been God who had made the whole escape possible, then He must have a purpose for why He did it. He must have a purpose for me.

I had been brought up in a conservative Christian family, but during the war I had not thought very much about God, and in combat I had never considered the possibility that I might die and face my Creator. Unfortunately, I couldn't connect these thoughts on the hill to my life, and soon they drifted from my mind like smoke in the wind until five years later when I faced myself.

I first went to the farm whose address I had memorized, with the hopes of meeting the others. I was received very warmly and so was my friend Tuennes, who arrived the next day. As for our other two comrades, we never saw them again, and I never discovered their fate.

The rest of our escape was not as dangerous as it had been. First we had to get into the American occupation zone. We needed documents and permission to go from one occupation zone to the other, which we didn't have; but apparently no one had them. The train, full of people, left in the direction of Salzburg. About half a mile before the demarcation line to the American zone, the train stopped. Everyone proceeded off the train and walked through a small forest to the other side of the border, where the train would be waiting for us. Everyone got on the train again, and before I knew it we were in Salzburg.

In Salzburg I found some former German soldiers who now drove trucks for the American Army. One of them had to transport potatoes to units in Bavaria allowing several of us to hide in the back of the truck between the potatoes. Then the driver picked up an American soldier to take him over the border, and that was it. Now we were in Germany. We got through the British and French controls in their respective occupation zones without any real problems and Tuennes left me in the French zone to join his family. One night I was pulled from the coal train on which I was riding by an American soldier. Nearby German prisoners of war had escaped from their camp, and he suspected me to be one of them. I had nothing to prove that I was not, but he simply let me climb back onto the train.

I did not know what had happened to my family. We had lived in Sudetenland, again called Czechoslovakia and occupied by the Red Army. So, I went to Bad Oeynhausen, located between Duesseldorf and Hannover, where my grandmother lived, thinking she might know something about my parents. Bad Oeynhausen, however, had become the headquarters of the British Army, and most people living there, including my grandmother, had been expelled from their homes. I found her not very far away, in a home for elderly people in Bielefeld. She told me that my father had been taken away by the Soviet army, and my mother, my sister Sibylle and my brother Burchard were ten miles away in Halle, the city where we were born.

I found them in Halle. My family didn't know what had happened to me, and since my grandmother told me that my mother had a heart problem and must not be agitated, I decided to prepare her gently for my return.

At that time in 1945, in the middle of defeat and despair, people helped each other in whatever way they could. So, I stopped a man in the street whom I didn't even know and asked him to prepare my mother for the arrival of her son. He went into the house where my mother had an apartment up in the attic, and prepared, not my mother, but the owner of the house who lived on the ground floor. This kind lady came out immediately, brought me into her kitchen, offered me food, and then climbed up the staircase to prepare my mother. Then I heard the noise my mother made nearly falling down the staircase rushing to meet me, overwhelmed with joy.

We had lost all our possessions in Freiwaldau, and my mother, sister and brother had started new lives as refugees in the city of our birth, but without the Nazis. At the same time, nearly 20 million refugees from East Germany and Eastern Europe were pouring into the small western part of the country. All of us were accommodated.

Under the cease-fire agreement for the Yugoslavia theatre, 200,000 German soldiers in Yugoslavia were promised, by the signatures of the Soviet High Command, that they could go home if they laid down their arms. Instead of going home, all of them landed in prisoner of war camps. Only half of them actually returned after several years of slave labor which, by the way, was forbidden by the Geneva Convention. One hundred thousand men perished, many by mass-executions. Fifty percent casualties was the highest percentage of German prisoners of war losing their lives in any country. In the Soviet Union 1,335,000 prisoners of war from a total of 3,060,000 perished. Only German crimes were prosecuted by the so-called justice of the victors. Nothing like this, however, happened in the three camps I was in; perhaps it was another miracle even before the escape began?

CHAPTER TWO

NAZI POWER

How Was It Possible?

"HOW WAS IT possible?" That was the question that haunted me after the war. Millions of people still ask that question today. If we could have said that Hitler was a person very different from all other human beings perhaps we could have stopped asking. If we could have said that he came from another planet, landed here to conquer people with brutal force, and then with the help of some other ruthless people committed his atrocities maybe that would have answered it. Maybe then a German like me could shrug his shoulders and say, "there is nothing I could have done. I have nothing to do with the whole disgrace."

One could also point to the various causes which led to Nazi power—the Versailles Treaty, the millions of unemployed in Germany at the beginning of the thirties, and the growing internal Communist threat. However, it wouldn't be an explanation; it would only be an excuse.

For non-Germans the easiest explanation would be to define National Socialism entirely as a German affair, which does not reflect on anybody else. That, of course, would also miss the point and fall short of an explanation. Because, if it were true, why then are Nazi philosophy, judicial corruption, and Nazi inspired laws steadily gaining ground in the main bastion of freedom in the world, the United States? The substance of freedom is being subverted by abandoning truth and establishing relativism. Jubilation about the progress of freedom and democracy around the world simply rings shallow in my ears. For I see the same things here that I saw in Germany during the rule of the Nazis.

Nazi stands for National Socialist. A Socialist represents Socialism, which is not Fascism. Whoever thinks that the Nazis are Fascists, as many intelligent people including professional journalists in America do, is brainwashed by the Soviets who want to distance themselves from the Nazis and who launched that lie during the war. Socialism is on the left and not on the right; National Socialism is but one of many different branches of a rotten tree. It is a moral perversion.

It was another German, of whom I am not very proud, Karl Marx, who defined this godless philosophy. Marxism is incompatible with Christian teachings and built on the concept that man is good but corrupted by society. By "society," Marx and his followers mean others, not themselves. Marxism, like terrorism, builds on hatred, greed and envy. They pretend to fight to change society, but in reality, Marxists are fighting for themselves first, using any means at their disposal. Listening to some of the American liberals, many of them rich, one must realize that they are hardcore Socialists, marshalling resentment, envy, and ambition for power just as Hitler did.

Marxist/Leninist Socialists have murdered hundreds of millions of people and have contributed nothing to the progress of humanity. Jesus Christ on the other hand, taught the world that a man is fallen because of his sinful human nature. He showed that moral change, repentance, restitution, and salvation through Him will lead to a new man and new nations. Christianity is based on love for God and for your neighbor, but that was not at the heart of the Nazi government, where the godlessness of the Nazi disaster was made possible by the evil concept of separation between government and God. Their refusal to apply absolute moral standards to human behavior, government procedures, and social structures and instead, acquire power with lies, disregarding the rights of others is godless and readily led to the dictatorship of relativism, (as Pope Benedict XVI so eloquently put it). It is godlessness again which threatens the world of today and our freedom. This book will define the issue and explain how to confront it.

THE CHARACTER OF HITLER

The Nazi philosophy and related atrocities grew from perverse characters. The people who were responsible for what happened didn't know the difference between right and wrong, and defined good as everything that served their own interest. They had no respect for the rights of others and had an arrogant contempt for human life.

Ironically, Hitler represented the fears, anxieties, resentments, hatreds, and hopes of millions of people. His characteristics were intolerance, lust for revenge, lack of generosity, and naked materialism. Author Allan Bullock described him as vain, full of hatred, touchy, moody, a person without standards, without roots, without scruples, and without family and home. Throughout his life he knew how to take advantage of others through lies, tricks, and distortions. Unable to admit his own mistakes, he presented himself as the fulfillment of justice, the savior of Germany, and as the leader to greatness for all Germans. He not only mobilized the fears, resentments, and ambitions of the German people, but also their patriotism channeling it all into his schemes. He was able to give young people a personal and national purpose, and challenge them to give their lives to the greatness of their country. At the same time he gave aimless people direction and a reason for living. Millions fell for it, blinded to its underlying evil. The idea that the German race was the best and most of the others were inferior to them struck a nerve in a large part of a nation filled with very uncertain people.

According to many sources, Hitler was a homosexual, which might explain how a man who had no social background got into the top social circles in Berlin. Samuel Ingram explains in his book "Germany's National Vice," that homosexuality was at the root of the sadistic cruelty in the concentration camps. Among the Nazi leaders known to be homosexual were Ernst Roehm, leader of two million storm troopers, SS General- Lieutenant Reinhard Heydrich, number two in the SS hierarchy and the head of the Berlin police.

THE NAZIS FIRE MY FATHER

In my family we detested the Nazis, but not so much because of their philosophy, we didn't really study the nonsense they declared to be divine revelation. I don't remember reading Hitler's book or the books of the top Nazis. We didn't like the kind of people who had suddenly become the most powerful section of German society. Children even looked at them suspiciously.

My parents knew more about the evil but couldn't discuss the matter with us children until we were older. Nazis in general were small-minded, revengeful, thought they knew everything better while they forced their party line on all others, and expected praise for Hitler as the fulfillment of German history. Everyone learned very quickly that it was not advisable to express a different opinion than that of the Nazis.

I remember the day they took power very well, it was January 30, 1933, and I was 7 years old. The very next morning our Nanny came walking through our playroom furiously muttering, "Now this painter made it after all!" The painter was Hitler who earlier in his life painted walls of houses and similar objects. Hitler's father Alois was the son of Maria Anna Schickelgruber, and born out of wedlock. It was said that Alois' father was a Jew. Alois later adopted the surname Hitler. According to rumors, he had beaten his son Adolf every day. Hatred of his father and rejection of his grandfather were part of Hitler's early life. Now this man had become Chancellor of Germany.

My father was the equivalent of a County Commissioner, a Landrat, who was the administrative head of a determined area. His local government office was in Halle, Westphalia, in the northwest of Germany, where we four children were born. A Landrat was not elected like a County Commissioner in the USA; instead he was a civil servant, appointed by the government.

As soon as the Nazis were in power, they established a party structure throughout Germany, which was supposed to ensure that Nazi philosophy and rules were applied. The party equivalent to a Landrat was a Kreisleiter, an area leader. The equivalent to a mayor was an Ortsgruppenleiter, a city group leader. The Nazi representative in the 1965 musical *The Sound of Music,* as well as the fanatic young man presented excellent characteristics of the mindset of the Nazis who tried to force their ways on the people from 1933 until the end of the war.

My father was approached and asked to join the Nazi Party, the National Socialist German Workers Party, (NSDAP, National-Sozialistische Deutsche Arbeiter Partei). As the name clearly shows, the Nazis were not a radical right-wing party, as the Cambridge Encyclopedia states. Nor was it a fascist party as the same Encyclopedia claims in another description.

It was an extreme left-wing Socialist party with a Marxist/Leninist philosophy. Their enemies were the same enemies that the Communists struggled with but were simply spun differently with different names. For instance, what the Communists called "capitalist" the Nazis called a "plutocrat"; what the Communists called a "classless society," the Nazis called "community of the people." A week before the invasion of the Soviet Union in 1941, Hitler explained to his top generals that he was going to bring real Socialism to the Soviet people. Joseph Goebbels, Hitler's chief liar, had said earlier, "We are really Communists. That is why we state in the name of our party that we are a worker's party."

I was 8 years old when my father rejected the proposition to join the party and was promptly fired afterwards. However, since he was a civil servant with a number of legal rights, they couldn't simply throw him out of the system. Instead, he was transferred to another job in a remote corner of Germany, Aurich in Ostfriesland, close to the North Sea. And since other civil servants with similar convictions as my father were there for the same reason, my parents found many friends with whom they could talk openly.

It didn't take very long before people realized they had to be careful with what they said however, because they could be betrayed to the Gestapo, the Secret State Police (Geheime Staats Polizei). Things had already degenerated to the point where criticizing the regime could land people in a concentration camp. As a result, a sort of social schizophrenia was born in Nazi society, people said what was expected in public, but at home and in a circle of close friends, they said what they really thought.

Soon, the Gestapo was everywhere. Professionally and materially, my father lost when the Nazis took over, but in Aurich he had the advantage of less exposure to Nazi interference than he would have had in Halle.

It shocks me to hear how much double talk there is already in the United States. As the result of an atmosphere created in part by the socialist media (although they bristle at the term), politicians who aren't socialist but don't want to lose votes yield to the wrong standards. There are millions of Americans who do the same, blindly following a political pied piper to their leisurely destruction.

THE CONSEQUENCES OF WORLD WAR I

My parents had resided in Halle for ten years prior to Hitler's ascent to power. They married in 1923 during the worst of times after World War I. Germany was devastated by hyperinflation as a result of the reparations owed to the victorious nations. The financial fallout was so severe that one billion marks were worth a mere U.S. dollar. And while ordinary people struggled desperately with a listing economy, it was boom time for big business and foreign investors.

Things were so bad at one point that my father was paid twice a day. Since our home was adjacent to his office in the same building, my mother would meet him there when they paid his salary. She had to fill a suitcase with the paper money he received, and then run into town to see what she could purchase for that money. I shall never forget the story of when the only thing her full suitcase of money could buy was toilet paper! Even today, I don't understand how people or businesses could function under such conditions. The middle class was nearly eliminated and how a person living on a fixed pension survived remains a mystery to me.

At the same time, there were civil war conditions erupting in various parts of the country. The Soviet leadership thought that through the growing strength of the German Communist Party and like-minded organizations, they would harvest Germany like a ripe fruit. However, the army and right wing paramilitary organizations, comprised mostly of veterans, prevented them from doing so.

Hitler was not the only one to refer to the so-called peace Treaty of Versailles as dictate. Germans were not allowed to participate in the deliberations in Paris and were told at the end, in June 1919, what they had to sign. All participants tried to get as much as they could from the defeated nations. Germany lost 1/7 of her territory and 1/10 of her population to Poland, Italy, France, Belgium, and Denmark and Austria were dismembered and the Sudetenland was made part of Czechoslovakia. Nobody bothered to ask the population what it wanted.

Poland claimed Upper Silesia because of its rich coalmines. A referendum of the population, mostly Germans, showed support for German rule. Nevertheless, by way of a clever partitioning of the area, Poland got 90 percent of the coal. In Versailles, and later in the "Treaty" with Austria in Saint-Germain-en-Laye and Trianon, and the treaty of Sevres with Turkey, the victors dismantled the central European and Middle Eastern political structures and created countless new nations through French Premier Minister Clemencau and British Prime Minister Lloyd George. These nations were created according to their victors own interests and not according to the realities and wishes of the populations. Democratic politicians always think of the next election and are usually unable to think in historical or long-range terms. Thus, the seeds for further conflicts were planted bringing a bitter harvest in due course.

The American president, Woodrow Wilson, was bewildered by the ferocity with which the Europeans fought for small pieces of land. He could not enforce his conviction that no person and no nation should be forced against their wills into a foreign political structure.

German leaders felt cheated since they had trusted that President Wilson's 14 points would be implemented. Presented to the Congress of the United States in January 1918, it was because of these 14 points that an undefeated Germany surrendered in November of that same year. The commitment to the self-determination of people and nations was incorporated into the "Treaty" of Versailles but as usual political double talk prevailed, and the principle had no part in the final arrangements.

The United States Senate, correctly interpreting the consequences of these arrangements, refused to ratify the document. To add insult to injury, in addition to the loss of land Germany was forced to sign a statement of guilt for starting the war and had to accept a murderous financial burden for reparations that put its economy in a tailspin.

I consider World War I as a European civil war between so-called Christian nations of Western society whose political leaders had nothing to show in terms of biblical motives as a basis for political decisions. Arrogance, lust for power, and stupidity by everyone involved led to the war. The same spirit of hatred, lust for revenge, greed, and indifference toward ordinary people was built into the Versailles Treaty, and created the conditions for another confrontation.

Christianity had become by and large a personal affair for those who believed in it, but was no longer a motivation for establishing justice, creating a society built upon its moral principles, or treating your enemy according to God's command to love your neighbor as you love yourself. If American and multinational forces had treated Iraq in the same way, they would have taken over its oil fields to compensate themselves for their efforts, and left the population to their own devices. Instead they created a democratically elected government and are helping the nation to stand on its own feet.

OUR FAMILY LIFE IN NAZI GERMANY

In spite of the oppressive surroundings, our family led a happy life, and we children had fun, parties, and even street fights with other children. I remember a number of incidents such as smoking some cigarettes when I was seven and feeling so miserable afterwards that I could not hide the fact from my mother. The tree we always used to climb is still there to this day, and I can still picture my little sister sitting on the pillar of the huge door leading to the parking area of my father's office building as she spit at the pedestrians strolling down the street beneath her.

My older brother Asche and I once made a bet to see who could hold a burning match in his hand the longest. We asked Sibylle to get us some matches from the kitchen. As she handed them over, she never dreamed that their tiny flickering flame would grow into an inferno that burnt the barn to the ground. The bet was off and to our amusement it was Sibylle, not my brother and I, who was punished for the misdeed because it was she who supplied us with the matches. It was difficult for her to endure three brothers; we were not easy and even made it clear when we disapproved of her friends.

It was not all humorous however. Once when my parents took us to visit friends, my youthful curiosity got the best of me and I jammed one of my fingers into the gear system of a machine. The result was not pretty as the top of my finger was almost completely severed remaining attached only by a patch of dangling skin. Strangely, I felt no pain as I ran to the house where my parents were visiting a trail of blood splattered behind me. And as I approached the door, I got a brainstorm and started to cry, pretending that I was in excruciating pain to impress everybody and garner his or her sympathy. Ultimately I had to have surgery and thankfully the physicians managed to reconstruct my finger.

Life went on bringing the usual ups and downs. We enjoyed many birthday parties and to my delight they always served traditional sand-wiches with cold cuts and cakes. I just didn't have much of a sweet tooth and ate my fill of sandwiches.

Most memorable was an invitation my parents received to watch the yearly hunting of wild horses on the nearby estate of the Duke of Schaumburg-Lippe, who had been the reigning monarch until the end of WWI. My great-grandfather, Carl von Campe, had been the top civil servant of that state.

Asche and I accompanied our parents, and were even allowed to attend the dinner in the castle of the prince after the hunt. Asparagus was in season and my mother suspected it would be part of the dinner menu for the 60 or so guests. Keenly aware that I didn't like asparagus, my parents strongly advised me to allow the waiter to serve me at least one asparagus or I would be severely punished. I promised I would.

I can still see the huge doors of the banquet hall slowly open and the servants coming in with mounds of asparagus on their enormous silver serving plates. Knowing I would never keep my promise, I avoided even looking in the direction of my mother. When the silver plate was held before me, the cheerful hum of the table talk ground to a cold, still halt as my piercing voice could be heard around the table to the furthest corner of the hall, "I don't eat asparagus!" My parents froze! When I dared to glance at them, the fury in my mother's eyes could have melted steel.

The next morning, instead of breakfast, my mother served me a full plate of asparagus, with the warning that I was not allowed to get up until I had eaten all of it. Four hours later I left the table a little queasy, and a lot wiser.

The von Campes are a noble family with our pedigree reaching back to the year 1075. Our family motto is engraved on the shield of our coat of arms reading: "Sola bona quae honesta" (Good is only what is honorable).

My grandfather, Friedrich von Campe, was a three star general and a division commander in WWI. Concerned, generous, and always friendly, he was the opposite of what foreigners normally conceive as a German military official. We loved to be with him and with grandma, who was small, dainty, and always a little preoccupied.

My other grandfather, Hans Wesener, was quite different. My mother's father, he was president of the railway system of Lower Saxony, formerly a kingdom until in 1866. The ruling Welfen family has provided many princes to Britain. He had an authoritarian character and was domineering subjecting everyone to his anger.

When he shouted at someone, his voice could be heard throughout the whole house. He struck fear in all our hearts, but never shouted at my grandmother, whom he loved dearly. She knew how to handle him, and behind his back, always tried to repair the damage he did. Of course, he also tried to subjugate my mother, but never really succeeded. She believed in the freedom and independence of a person, and very often, to the horror of grandma, bluntly told her father when she disagreed with him.

My mother treated the Nazis in the same way. After we had settled in Aurich, functionaries of the party would come to our home from time to time, though I don't recall why. They had to discuss business with my father, I suppose. My mother confronted them right away and told them how wrong they were in their thinking, and that what they were doing was bad. Once they had left, my father would implore her, nearly on his knees, to keep quiet. "Don't you realize that you put your whole family in danger?" My mother remorsefully promised to be more careful the next time, but when the next time came, she'd let it fly again and tell them what she thought. Though they should have, the Nazis never retaliated against my mother and father.

It was very difficult for my parents to know what was up or what was down. All the media coverage in Germany was tainted. There were two foreign radio stations with news in the German language, BBC London and Beromuenster in Switzerland. My father listened regularly to Beromuenster even though listening to foreign broadcasts was strictly forbidden and you could pay with your life if you were caught.

The Nazis were especially cunning and always tried to get information from children about their parents. Knowing this, my father was careful to always listen to the Swiss radio broadcast late at night. Once, for whatever reason, my sister Sibylle could not sleep and came down to the living room where my father was listening to the radio. The color drained from his face as he looked up and saw her because he knew that children were prone to fall for the wiles of the Nazis and innocently give their parents away. Thankfully, nothing happened that time.

In 1936 my parents went to Switzerland and visited our friends, the Steinfels family. It was like a breath of fresh air for them. They got a firsthand exposure to what other nations thought about the Nazis and developments in Germany. The Swiss were in a very difficult geographical position between Germany and Italy, but they had a formidable army and nearly invincible mountain defenses. Every Swiss male then, as is the case today, had a rifle at home and was available within 24 hours in case of an attack. Hitler would have liked to occupy Switzerland but his generals cautioned that the only certainty of an attack on Switzerland was a tremendous body of casualties for the German army. He wisely abstained. Even today when I visit the son of my parents' friends in Zuerich, the first thing I see when I open the front door of the house is a machine gun mounted and ready to shoot! There must be a lack of liberals over there.

The main concern of my parents was to defend the integrity of their children and to save us from Nazi corruption. Although the danger was so great that they couldn't risk discussing those matters with us, they tried desperately to prevent our thinking from being subtly subjugated.

The Nazis had a parallel, elite education system, The National Political Education Program. They selected young people to enter the system to be trained for leadership positions in the Nazi state. My elder brother Asche was selected and invited when he was 16. That became a nightmare for my parents. It was the last thing they wanted. The "invitation," in reality, had the nature of an order or directive which was very difficult to reject. Ultimately, the only way they could keep Asche out of Nazi hands was with medical arguments. There was something wrong with his heart, which they blew out of proportion with the help of a doctor, and as a result he didn't have to enter that program.

Mother and father ferociously defended our family without fully understanding what was happening. From the very beginning, the Nazis recruited the youth into their camp as part of a long-term ideological program for their power. They were out to destroy the family nucleus, to wrestle the children away from their parents, brainwash them, and make them Nazis. That meant removing God and making Hitler their idol. It was because of the war that their purpose did not come to fruition. They also had a program under way in which they selected Aryan girls and paired them over a number of days in carefully prepared surroundings with Aryan men. The idea was to create children for the "Fuehrer." Women, like my mother, who had four or more children were decorated with medals. Hitler needed soldiers. And though she wanted to, she couldn't reject the honor.

It is important for the American reader to understand that on the surface, these programs of seducing young people appear to be a moral issue, but the real issue or purpose behind the seduction was to acquire *power* for a totalitarian ideology. Consequently, I know what the ACLU is after.

Those who love God and freedom must know that if they do not deal with the issue of power but only the issue of morality, they will not get anywhere. They can only slow down the process of being taken over when the social structures are simultaneously emptied of God's moral absolutes. Morality is the battlefield where the struggle for power is being waged. In former centuries armies fought wars on the frontlines. But times have changed and today's frontlines include universities, newspaper offices, subverted political parties, issues like the "right" to have sex and use condoms, the "right" to have an abortion without consent of the parents, and the "right" to same-sex marriages.

It is the soul of America that is being fought for, not its physical territory. America lost the Vietnam War, at home in the battle for the will of the nation, not in Vietnam itself. We face the same type of ferocious attacks today, as the darkest of forces strive to prevail over the American spirit where its coup cannot be seen and stopped. Their strategy is designed to end the war in Iraq the same way, by manipulating the thinking of the people.

The reader must also understand that people who live for themselves and their own pleasures, discard God's Commandments, and thus, are no match for militant ideologies. Immorality and godlessness are the same. If people don't stand for something they will fall for anything. America used to be a conviction driven nation. Sadly, these convictions have been supplanted by a pleasure-driven self-absorption and our honor lies fallen in our streets.

As every other youngster, I was forced to enter the Hitler Youth. Hitler eliminated all other youth organizations shortly after he took power, and by law, parents were forced to send their children into the Hitler Youth organization. Ten- to thirteen-year-old children were placed in the "Young People" program, while the fourteen- to seventeen-year-olds were placed in the standard Hitler Youth. It was all automatic, no one passed "Go" or collected their $200 and the reprisal for not complying was severe.

There is very little to report about those years except that we met twice a week, on Wednesday afternoons and Saturday mornings. Sometimes there were special events on Sundays, to prevent us from going to church. It was simply part of our life, like school. While we didn't question it, it still didn't have any special meaning and thankfully, I never had to attend bigger events outside of our town.

When I was interviewed in 2003 by the Holocaust Documentation and Education Center in Miami, I was asked whether I had been proud to be a member of the Hitler Youth. "For Heaven's sake," I answered, "why would I be proud? I was proud about my family and of Germany."

I sang Nazi songs, like the Banner Song, without thinking. This song stated, "Our banner flutters before us; our banner represents the new era; and our banner leads us to eternity; yes, our banner means more to us than death." Hitler, of course, described what he thought young people should be like: "slim and slender, fast as a greyhound, tough as leather and hard as Krupp steel." At a mass rally of youth in 1934 he said: "We do not want this nation to become soft. Instead, it should be hard and you will have to harden yourself while you are young. You must learn to accept deprivations without ever collapsing. In you, Germany will live on, and when nothing is left of us you will have to hold up the banner, which some time ago we lifted out of nothingness."

Previously, in 1933, he had stated: "My program for educating youth is hard. Weakness must be hammered away. In my castles of Teutonic Order a youth will grow up and the world will tremble. I want a brutal domineering, fearless, cruel youth. Youth must be all that. It must bear pain. There must be nothing weak and gentle about it. The free, splendid beast of prey must once again flash from its eyes…That is how I will eradicate thousands of years of human domestication…That is how I will create the New Order."

I don't remember indoctrination sessions about race superiority or anything like that. We lived in small cities and that probably saved us from being brainwashed by all of Hitler's ideas. In school we were told about German national history, how good and special we had always been, the victories we had achieved, how unjust the dictates of the Treaty of Versailles were, and how Hitler and the Nazi party gave Germany the right kind of leadership. Degrading remarks about God and the Jews had also become part of the system, but I didn't really think very much about it. As most other youngsters, I was not very interested in Nazi affairs, but rather, I did what I wanted. Generally speaking, we were like other youth enjoying sports, competitions, singing, marching, excursions, field-exercises, etc. I don't have any real memories about outstanding Nazi characteristics, but again, like many of my contemporaries, I took great pride in Germany, not the Nazis.

We didn't escape unscathed, however, and in time the Nazi ideology infested our greater family. The conflict was so sharp that we were split into two factions so antagonistic that we did not even talk to each other: the Nazis and the Anti-Nazis. My family detested the Nazis and saw through the way these pinheaded people with no education tried to impose their arrogant views on everybody. The Nazis in our extended family were led by my uncle Hans, my mother's brother, a colonel, and my uncle Adolf, my mother's brother in law who became a highly decorated general. I don't think they committed crimes but they did fit the description of what makes a person a Nazi. A Nazi is somebody who accepts the Nazi ideology and Hitler's opinions as his own set of values and acts accordingly. My uncles went to war for their ideology, for revenge of WWI, and to pursue world conquest. I went to war to defend my fatherland.

At the 1938 conference in Munich between Hitler, French Prime Minister Daladier, and British Prime Minister Neville Chamberlain, the Sudetenland was returned from Czechoslovakia to Germany. The 3.5 million people who lived there were German speaking Austrians who had fallen victim to the Treaty of Saint-Germain-en Laye in 1919. Without asking them, it herded these poor Austrians like cattle to a new state where they didn't want to live, and made their territory part of Czechoslovakia. Becoming a badly treated minority in a country that was not theirs, they were understandably enthusiastic to become German citizens. Their joy, however, was not because they were Nazis, rather, because they returned to their national environment.

My father was sent by the government to Freiwaldau/Graefenberg, a beautiful Sudeten-German city in the middle of the Altvater Mountains, to take over the administration of that specific area. He was again a Landrat. The job was supposed to last half a year, and then was to be taken over by a local, but he was one of two German Landrats who, on request from the population, were asked to stay on. We joined him in the spring of 1939.

This was even better for my father as far as his dealings with the

Nazis were concerned. He didn't have to face the grumpy, "knowing-everything-better" party functionaries that made life difficult in what we called the "Altreich," Germany before 1938. People there, including the official Nazi representatives, were an easy-going and friendly people. If they couldn't agree on something between themselves, they came to my father (much to his amusement) and asked him to sort things out.

We children had mostly a good time. It began with school. We left Aurich in April of 1939 when the school year was over. In Freiwaldau, however, the school year ended when the summer vacations began. There was also a different study plan. We had started with Latin when we were 10 in the "Sexta," the first year of the gymnasium. In Freiwaldau, Latin started in the "Unter Tertia," the fourth year when you were 13. I was, without effort, the best, the apple of the Latin teacher's eye, and immediately advanced to the head of the class. All of us children were moved ahead again to the next class in July. It was wonderful. I graduated from school when I was only 16 years old and by that time was the only male left in the class, everybody else was in the army.

We four children consisted of the two tall ones, Asche and I, and the two small ones, Sibylle and Burchard. The main difference in our upbringing at that point was simply in the hour when we had to be in bed at night. To their great annoyance, Sibylle and Burchard had to go to bed earlier.

During wintertime it was cold and snowy in Freiwaldau. We learned how to ski, and we could even use our skis from home directly onto the mountain's ski areas. It was awesome, but not without its risks. Shortly before I was done with school, I hit a tree while going down the mountain at a great speed causing my right knee to be filled with fluid. I could walk only with great difficulty and no doctor knew what it was. Several months later, the injury was diagnosed as a torn cartilage requiring surgery and several months of rehabilitation. Medicine in those days was not what it is today, which added to my frustrated desire to enter the army before the war was over even though I was but seventeen-years-old. Looking back at this delay, especially in the context of my escape, I have to believe that the hidden hand of God reached in to my destiny through this injury. If I had entered the army in 1942 instead of 1943, I most likely would have been sent to the Russian front. The chances of survival there were considerably less than those in Yugoslavia, and to be a prisoner of war in Siberia would have virtually assured my death.

We used alternative fuels during the war. My father had an official car which came with the office. It ran on normal gas. We also had a smaller, personal car which was fueled by burning wood in a small oven attached to the end of the car, a technical process I cannot remember. IG Farben, the huge chemical company which was dismantled after the war, developed a process whereby coal was chemically processed into fuel. Germany had plenty of coal but no oil. The process was so effective that during the entire war this fuel enabled Germany to keep trucks, planes, and ships running. Additionally, though the method held a German patent, South Africa used this procedure during the years of international sanctions. The South African company SASOL AFRICAN (SSL) produced the fuel from coal.

Since the United States is so dependent on foreign oil and its prices are skyrocketing I ask myself why is there no attempt to use this procedure in light of the nearly unlimited coal reserves in this country. According to a German intelligence officer, who at this writing is still alive, IG Farben and Standard Oil made an agreement to respect the other's territory in the 1930s. IG Farben would not enter the US market, and Standard Oil made reciprocal concessions. The latter did not like the idea of coal displacing oil. They then opened joint offices and agreed contractually that, should there be a war and Western democracies win, the offices would be located in Switzerland—and should Germany win, the offices would be located in Holland.

Because Pennsylvania is rich in coal reserves, its Governor explored this process in 2005. A daunting proposition, his findings were encouraging enough to make preparations to take on the powerful oil cartel.

To date the fate of program is unknown, but its potential begs its share of questions.

My parents remained in Freiwaldau until the end of the war. By that time, all of us children had already left the city. In early 1945, my younger brother Burchard was called into the army at the age of 17, while my sister Sibylle found herself on a farm in Thueringen.

THE PERSECUTION OF THE JEWS

The persecution of the Jews began in 1933 right after the Nazis came to power. Kicked off with a Nazi campaign that prohibited Germans from buying anything from a Jewish business, storm troopers took up positions in front of Jewish stores and prevented potential customers from entering. Slowly, but systematically, our Jewish citizens were marginalized and stripped of their rights. Later on, all Jews had to publicly identify themselves with a yellow Star of David on their clothing. All of this was very cruel and dehumanizing. Quite a number of these Jews were officers and soldiers who risked their lives fighting for Germany in World War I.

Every German saw this discrimination of a helpless minority and knew what was being done. There was no outcry by the churches, there were no protests on the streets, nor was there any resistance by society. It is an appalling story of a nation of cowards and appeasers, which to my shame, I was part of, even as a boy. I do not remember ever hearing our church make any reference to the blatantly brutal and godless treatment of the Jewish people.

The population of Aurich at that time consisted of about 6,000 people. More than a thousand were Jews. Our neighbor was Jewish and we played with the children. But when I was 12 or 13 years old, I remember marching with a group of youth through the Jewish section of the city singing anti-Jewish songs. Even today, I am very ashamed of what I did, trampling on other people who were suffering.

In November of 1938 I was awakened one morning when it was still dark by a friend who pounded the window of my bedroom. "The synagogue is on fire," he shouted, and "you must not miss this spectacle." The synagogue was right in front of our house on a hill, and I could see everything. We didn't think of the people or their horror, we only felt excitement. That day, the Jews were taken out of their houses and assembled on a huge soccer field where they were crammed on to trucks and carried away to face unspeakable terrors. We were simply told that they were taken to work camps.

The pure inhumanity, of which I was a part, still makes me shudder. It is true that we, like most Germans, did not know of the Holocaust until after the war. But all of us to various degrees saw what was done to the Jews before the Holocaust which was cruel and evil. At that time, my father was not in Aurich anymore, and when my mother and we children left in spring of 1939 for Freiwaldau, the whole matter slipped into the back of my mind to be conveniently forgotten.

We did not see the writing on the wall and maybe we did not want to. I believe only my father was always aware of what happened and in a telling remark some two years before the war ended he lamented to my mother, "We can no longer wish that Germany wins this war." As a patriot and decorated World War I Veteran, who loved his country and had a son in the army, it was a terrible and painful conclusion for him to reach. He had saved in Freiwaldau several Jews and Czechs from the Nazi machine.

From 1933 on, Jews were barred from the economy, their businesses were plundered or destroyed, and eventually they were expelled from the universities, publishing houses, and banks. In 1935 they lost their rights of citizenship. After the widespread destruction of Crystal Night with its synagogues burnings, beatings, and vandalism, persecution intensified until it climaxed with the Holocaust—the unwarranted suffering and murder of six million innocent people.

The story of a Jewish friend of mine, whom I met in the United States, is an example of what Jews went through in the Nazi days. Henry

Schuster's family lived in a small village, Sterbfritz, near Frankfurt. He was six years old when the Nazis took over. He lost his family in Nazi concentration camps. Only he and a sister survived. In his own words:

> Prior to 1933, Teacher Weidling felt very comfortable to as-
> sociate with the Jews. In fact, he would join several of them
> on many a Sunday afternoon at Michel Schuster's Café and
> play cards. In 1934 he joined the Nazi Party and became very
> belligerent to his former Jewish friends...He encouraged the
> students to harass us Jewish kids. We Jewish kids had to partic-
> ipate in the singing of anti-Jewish songs. One time, Weidling
> demanded that I sing solo the Horst Wessel song (the Nazi
> hymn). I didn't know the words, but he demanded I start sing-
> ing. As punishment he took his switch and hit me repeatedly
> on the palms of my hands. There was not a day that I didn't
> receive a whipping from him. He looked for an excuse. After
> school we Jewish kids were hassled and abused on our way
> home from school. Often they would yell abusive language at
> us. On many occasions I was stoned and attacked and beaten
> by the bullies. My former so-called friends the Kolebs were
> among the most hateful.

Early laws were passed that forbade Germans to buy from Jewish merchants. They also passed a law that absolved people and/or compa-nies of debts owed to Jews. Jewish people, however, were still required to pay their debts, forcing many Jewish businesses into bankruptcy. Jews were also not allowed to have stock certificates or government bonds and no German was allowed to work for a Jew. An uncle of my friend, therefore, had to sell his factory to one of his employees.

My friend's father sold his grocery store to a man named Kirst with payment in installments. First, Kirst stopped paying for the business, and then took over their house, without paying a cent. In like spirit, the mayor ordered each Jewish family to have a family member report to a road gang to crush stones to be spread on a street that needed repair.

As the persecution grew more severe, my friend was sent to an orphanage in another city. On November 10, the day after the Crystal Night, the children had lunch in the dining room. He later described the unthinkable events:

Several Jewish men from the neighborhood came to hide in the home. They were asked to go into the synagogue and make believe that they were attending a service. Then all hell broke loose. Several brown-shirt Nazis came looking for adults. They found the men in the synagogue and proceeded to beat them without mercy. They took the sacred Torahs from the Ark, tore them and trampled them on the floor. We could all hear what was going on. They came into the dining room and started swinging clubs at anyone in their path. They arrested the adult men and older boys and forced them to go with them.

Two days later Uncle Moritz showed up at the Alperstein to seek refuge. When I saw him I could not recognize him… Several hoods from another town had come to their house and had beaten him to a bloody pulp. He looked awful. When they thought he was dead they left…

The Holocaust was the climax of the persecution of the Jews. Not only did the Nazis murder 6 million Jews, but after having already stolen their property, they proceeded to take the gold from the teeth of the dead.

Shortly afterwards, my friend traveled to France within the framework of an international initiative of European countries to accept Jewish children from Germany. From France he reached the United States. In May 1944 he joined the United States Army, and eventually returned to Frankfurt as a soldier with the US army and proceeded to recuperate his family's property in Sterbfritz. In 2004 he was instrumental in erecting several monuments in his hometown to honor all of that town's Jews who were murdered during the Holocaust. Henry and his wife Anita organized the Holocaust Survivors Group of Southern Nevada and have been active in many Jewish organizations.

THE ROAD TO A TOTALITARIAN SOCIETY

The Nazi ideology was deliberately vague, enabling it to change according to strategic political purposes. When, in 1932, unemployment reached six million, Hitler's party received only 37 percent of the votes in the elections. He became chancellor in January 1933 as a result of an agreement with conservatives who thought they could control him. His first government included only two Nazis; one was the minister of Interior who controlled the police. Hitler immediately called for new elections in March to consolidate his power. Subsequently the Nazis burned down the Reichstag (Parliament), and Hitler blamed the communists for it in order to heighten the fears of the people and win their votes. His ascent into power and coercion of Germany into war later on were based on lies.

In the March election he received 44 percent of the vote and two days later, Parliament gave him unlimited power. The first concentration camp was opened in Dachau and filled with political adversaries. Communists and Socialists were expulsed from parliament and syndicates, and state governments within the German Republic were dissolved. Jews in the federal administration were dismissed, and workers were organized in the Nazi organization, as Deutsche Arbeitsfront (Front of German Workers), and the Trade Unions were dissolved. The road to dictatorship was open; it was just a matter of time now.

By the end of 1933, Hitler's first year in office, the SA, (Sturm Abteilung/storm troopers) had a whopping two million members. They got their name during the twenties when the Nazis entered the political arena on a large scale. In general, they were rowdies that had the task of silencing the opposition, an undertaking they excelled at. Their leader, Ernst Roehm, a known homosexual, was one of Hitler's closest friends, but he had become a rival and a threat to Hitler's power.

However, the army and the SS had misgivings leading the SS to organize an uprising in Munich. They blamed the SA for it, resulting in Hitler's order to execute Roehm as well as the top SA leaders. The government murdered about 300 other people they considered threats, including some leading Nazis, Conservatives, and a former chancellor. A month later, the President, Fieldmarschall Paul von Hindenburg, died. Hitler produced a falsified last will of von Hindenburg, in which he ratified Hitler as a person he fully trusted—another lie! This paved the way for Hitler to take over the presidency in addition to being head of the government. Hitler's administration was confirmed shortly afterwards by a referendum and supported by an overwhelming majority of an artfully brainwashed population. The Gestapo, part of the SS, became the German society's undisputed enforcer strong-arming obedience to Hitler and his high-level Nazi henchmen.

From that day on, officers and civil servants like my father had to swear a personal oath of allegiance to the "Fuehrer," a pledge that had far-reaching and unfortunate consequences later on in the war. We did not realize it then, but it also sealed the fate of my father. The point of no return had been reached on a grand scale and from that point on, even whispers of dissent were considered suicidal. All German citizenry was expected to be enthusiastic about the "outstanding achievements" of Hitler.

Later on Hitler accused the commander of the army, General Werner von Fritsch, of being a homosexual, which was another one of his lies devised to attain total power. Instead of fighting the issue, Fritsch resigned and Hitler made himself the commander of the army. He then dismissed the minister of defense, General Werner von Blomberg, and took over his position as commander-in-chief of all the armed forces. His power was absolute and he ensured that all essential information was channeled to him so that no one could grasp the complete picture of what was happening without his permission. His chief liar, spin doctor Joseph Goebbels, once explained that you don't need more than 10,000 people to control Germany or any nation of that size. You only need to occupy the switchboards of power transmission, and you have everyone following your orders. And that is exactly what they did. Hitler was a dictator in the literal sense of the word at the top of the food chain ruling a totalitarian structure with an iron fist.

Again, the Nazi ideology as such was rather vague and I always found it rather difficult to define the substance of it. I certainly do not remember ever being forced to proclaim a certain set of beliefs, and I don't think my father was. We were told to live our daily lives and leave the decisions for political developments to the Fuehrer. And because the character of a German tends to make him or her obedient to the government we tended to comply and suffer the consequences.

The permanent Nazi features of life in those years were the greatness of Germany, the ridicule of God, the denigration of the Jews, and the aggrandizement of the Aryan race. As unashamedly egregious as our nation became, I didn't grasp the significance of those features, and I don't remember having had any discussions on Nazi ideology. What we dealt with was an aspect of life, not of ideology, and the direction of the country was delivered to us, not in blatant training or indoctrination sessions, but subtly in school, films, and newspapers as part of reporting.

When interviewed for 4 ½ hours by the Holocaust Documentation and Education Center in Miami in 2003, the interviewer asked me several times for the contents and duration of the Nazi indoctrination sessions in the army. It took her some time to grasp the reality that there really was no Nazi indoctrination in the army. On the contrary, nobody who served in the armed forces—with exception of the SS divisions—could be in any political party at the same time. Since the NSDAP was the only party in existence, there was no party representative watching over soldiers as was done by the commissars of the communist party in the Red Army. We were the German army and not the Nazi Army. We didn't understand that our perceptions made no difference to them as long as we did what we were ordered to. The leadership of the armed forces was firmly in Hitler's grasp.

We didn't need to be indoctrinated. We fought from our own free will because we believed we were defending our country. The Nazi leaders were intelligent enough to know that trying to make Nazis out of us might compromise our commitment to fight. It would certainly have driven more army top brass into opposition to Hitler. He was quite satisfied that millions of soldiers led by their generals made his hidden purposes possible. The final blow to freedom was scheduled after victory in the war.

I never heard of Hitler's purpose to conquer the world, but I did hear him talking about justice for Germany. Hitler and his henchmen were perpetual liars. The shifting of their focus from big business to the workers, for instance, was a consequence of their tactical needs. They made the rules up as they went long and did whatever served them at the moment to achieve their strategic goals always articulating the necessary reasons. And whether those reasons were true or not was of no consequence.

The presence of the party in daily life intensified for my parents but not for us children. My father was practically compelled into membership of the Nazi Party and forced into the SS without being asked. I never saw him in an SS uniform and I don't think he participated in their activities. However Sibylle, my sister, remembers that he once came back from some event in his SS uniform and said to our mother, "Get this uniform off me. I feel like I have blood on my hands."

I know that in the foreign office from the time Joachim von Ribbentrop was foreign minister in 1937; all diplomats were obliged to be party members. Civil servants could have been subject to a similar government mandate. Right after I had reached the age of 18 in 1943, I was summoned to the party office in town. There I was informed by some party people that I had been transferred from the Hitler Youth to the NSDAP and I needed to sign the application. It was the last thing I wanted, but I didn't dare decline signing. Anyway, I knew that in a few weeks I would join the army and therefore, my membership would not be active. Nevertheless, I signed the application, and with that signature, cut a covenant with evil and committed an act of cowardice.

Hitler is known to have sworn to destroy the Christian religion and churches, but he didn't dare forbid them as he did with all other organizations. Therefore, he created the "German Christians," a measurable group of pastors and churches that promoted Nazi propaganda in religious language. When we went to our Lutheran church on Sundays in Freiwaldau, we often faced two Gestapo men near the entrance, writing down the names of those who entered the church and thereby intimidating them. It was certainly a threat to my father, a civil servant who was well aware of the danger, yet stayed faithful to his convictions. A heroic figure, in time he paid dearly to stay true to what he knew was true.

The Nazis embraced the concept of separation of church and state. They told us that we could pray and sing hymns as much as we liked at home and in the churches, but in society it wasn't the teachings of the Bible that mattered, but rather, their national socialist concepts and laws.

What they really meant therefore, was the separation of God and society, or maybe better put, God *from* society. That of course, is exactly what the American Civil Liberties Union (ACLU) is after today. They have been very successful in making Nazi concepts the law in America by distorting the intentions of the founding fathers and our Constitution.

The Nazis knew that God's moral absolutes were an obstacle to their total control because you can only manipulate morally weak people who care only for themselves. Therefore, the Christian religion and its moral absolutes had to be destroyed. During the first years of power and during the war, Hitler could only weaken their impact. The final destruction he had planned was meant to occur after the war was won. Like Hitler, the ACLU is also lying about their real purpose. Like

Hitler, the ACLU talks a good game yet it is their conduct, not their rhetoric that shows who they truly are.

"I promise you," Hitler told his inner circle, "that if I wanted to I could destroy the Church in just a few years. It is hollow, it is rotten and false through and through. One push and the whole structure would collapse. We should trap the preachers by their notorious greed and self-indulgence. We shall thus be able to settle everything with them in perfect peace and harmony. I shall give them a few years' reprieve. Why should we quarrel? They will swallow anything in order to keep their material advantage. The parsons will be made to dig their own graves; they will betray their God for us. They will betray anything for the sake of their miserable jobs and incomes."

The National Socialist ideologist, Alfred Rosenberg, described the Nazi themes in his book "The Myth of the 20th Century." He didn't have much to say other than describing history as a battle between the Aryan and the Semitic forces in the world. The Semitic forces included Christianity, which through Paul had been integrated into Judaism. He saw the Christian religion as propping up old women and weaklings.

Rosenberg preached that neither moral absolutes in law, nor absolute truth existed. According to him, right was defined by what serves the Aryan. The number two Nazi leader, Hermann Goering, described right as, "what serves the state." Hitler declared that in the battle for life, the strongest survive as they force their will upon the weak. In other words, the Nazis decided what was right and wrong and they enforced it. Thus their laws shifted as needed to impose their own power interests. The Nazi state was a dictatorship of relativism, an expression of godlessness. Any Communist state is the same, and what principle reigns in the church-going West? Winston Churchill said it best, "Right or wrong, my country!" The head of a multinational corporation would say, "right or wrong, my profit."

Nazi philosophy and the Nazi state were built on lies. The first lie came from each one of these imposters regarding their own character. They were dishonest about who they were and portrayed themselves as better than others. Most ridiculous! The next lie was that there was no God. Then as a logical continuation of the first lie, another one followed—that human value is subjective with some people being worth more than others. Of course this philosophy justified completely stripping the value of the Jews, regarding them as garbage, and treating them as such with no value whatsoever. That concept was expressed in the so-called Nurnberg Laws, which made it legal to rob the Jewish people of their legitimate rights. They literally became non-persons, similar to unborn babies in America and became subject to the ghastly consequences I described earlier. The result was the Holocaust—one of the modern world's most shocking manifestations of contempt for human life.

All of this happened because a vast segment of German society was godless and did not have the moral courage to stand up and protest. Instead, people preferred to remain willfully blind, indifferent, or silent to what we all saw was happening. There is a saying in Germany that the receiver of stolen goods is the same criminal as the thief. That applies also to what I am saying here. The Nazis committed the crimes, but could never have gotten away with them without appeasers inside and outside like Chamberlain and Daladier who made it possible.

Relativism may appear in different forms at different times in history and flourishes in different environments but there is an underlying reality in all forms of relativism—godlessness. Today godlessness is thriving as never before on a global scale and will inevitably lead to disaster if it isn't countered. I was forced to face godlessness up-close-and-personal in my own life after the war, a shattering confrontation which I will describe later in this book.

We have not spoken about the totalitarian character of Hitler's regime. I don't think I heard that word, nor would I have had any idea what it meant if I had. Although it hadn't been defined for us, we slid into a totalitarian regime via Hitler's stealth. It is a system in which the ruling government takes total control of the entire population. It is not an ordinary dictatorship in which one man or a group of few run a country without allowing any interfering by the opposition. Totalitarian rule goes a step further. It doesn't just control the policies, resources, and the direction of a country but also manipulates the thinking of the people to the system's policies.

Buying into the lies we were told, we were led right where Hitler wanted us to go; to war. As philosopher George Santayana warned, "Those who do not learn from history are doomed to repeat it." If in a democratic nation today such as ours, the government, a newspaper, or a political party lie to the people with regards as to what is happening and why, or twist the truth about the reasons for their decisions and actions, then they are leading their country toward a totalitarian environment. That is why lies are so dangerous. Lies destroy freedom. Liars, especially liars in civil government, are more dangerous than a suicide bomber. Even more dangerous than these are the liars in the media, for they shape the thinking and belief system of the nation.

Mind control also implied that thinking negatively about the controlling regime, in our case, Hitler and the Nazis, was a crime punishable by death. The crime was called "defeatism," a move by the government to brand opposition leaders into criminals and get rid of them. The Soviet purges in the thirties under Stalin showed the grim reality of this totalitarian distortion of law.

A totalitarian system is the installed dictatorship of relativism to use the definition of Pope Benedict XVI. All relativisms lead to that final stage and millions of Germans like me who adopted that mindset made the Nazi totalitarian system possible. It is the end form of state relativism.

CHAPTER THREE

THE BEGINNING OF WORLD WAR II

THE OFFICIAL VERSION

ON THE MORNING of September 1, 1939, addressing the members of the German Reichstag in Berlin (the token Nazi representatives in the Parliament), Hitler stated: "Today Polish regular soldiers have opened fire for the first time from our territory. Since 5:45am we are firing back." In his speech Hitler mentioned a total of 14 incidents at the border between Poland and Germany and vowed that they were incited by Poland.

On September 3, Britain and France declared war on Germany, honoring their pledge to support Poland after Germany had occupied Czechoslovakia in March of the same year.

World War II had begun. There was nothing, however, they could do to help Poland since their governments refused to listen to the German military intelligence when they tried to inform them of the gathering storm earlier.

WHAT REALLY HAPPENED?

On August 22, 1939, Hitler explained to the top commanders of the German armed forces that he was determined to go to war, if necessary, against the Western powers, although he didn't expect to. However, it would be necessary, he said, to destroy Poland. He also mentioned the need for new frontiers in order to achieve justice for 80 million Germans who, he argued, must have a secure existence. "I shall create the necessary propaganda reason to explain the beginning of the war. It doesn't matter whether it is credible or not. Nobody will ask the victor later on whether he spoke the truth."

Hitler, top SS leader Heinrich Himmler, and head of the internal security forces, (which included the Gestapo) SS Lieutenant-General Reinhardt Heydrich, had agreed upon a plan to draw Poland into war at the beginning of August 1939. The SS was authorized to execute the plan.

On the night of August 31 to September 1, 1939, three SS units that had been formed for an elite mission donned Polish uniforms and mobilized. The units then attacked the Radio Station Gleiwitz; the custom building Hochlinden; and the forester's house Pitchen, all located in Silesia close to the border on German territory. The code words for the operation were "Enterprise Tannenberg," and for the order to attack, "Grandmother died."

To add a touch of realism and demonstrate that there had been a battle, a number of political inmates held in the nearby concentration camp Sachsenhausen were murdered and outfitted in Polish uniforms than distributed around the three targets as fallen enemy combatants. One German civilian, Franz Honiok, who had done nothing wrong, but lived in the area, spoke Polish and was known to be friendly with the Poles, was arrested by the Gestapo, killed and left lying at the doorsteps of the radio station. His death was carried out to make people believe that he was the person who had given a victory speech over the radio. The bodies of these murdered people disappeared once the press had registered, and reported on them. The commandos quietly buried them in a mass grave.

Hitler lied, murdered, and started a war. I was 14 years old at that time. We only heard the official story, the party line, since the only media outlets, newspapers, and radio were controlled entirely by the

Nazis. When Britain and France entered the war two days later, it was clear to us that Germany was lined up against the same enemies they fought in World War I.

Our family detested the Nazis, but like millions of other Germans we believed their lies to be reality. Accordingly, we came to the conclusion that this was not a Nazi war but a national conflict against the same nations that had put us through the humiliation of the Versailles Treaty, destroyed our honor, and ruined our economy. We could not allow a recurrence of our fate in WWI. "First we shall win the war, and then we shall deal with the Nazis," we thought naïvely. When I became a soldier four years later I thought that I was defending my country, not the wanton slaughter of Jewish people. It was a terrible awakening after the war when I faced the atrocities of the Nazis including the Holocaust.

The beginning of World War II happened exactly the way I have reported here, but these are only the surface events. The underlying reality, however, began to present itself to me 11 years later.

CHAPTER FOUR

THE WAR

MY BROTHER FELL

THE WAR STARTED on September 1, 1939, only a few months after we had settled in Freiwaldau. Since we were located in a more remote corner of the country it didn't affect our daily life very much. We went to school, enjoyed our vacations, and of course listened to the news. The Polish campaign came to an end that same September and then there were no bigger military events until next spring when the Western front was opened and the Benelux countries and France were defeated and occupied.

We got used to what was called "Blitzkrieg"—decisive and fast military operations, ending in victory. Noteworthy events, such as the end of a battle of encirclement with the capture of some divisions or an enemy army were announced via radio as a news flash. They were always introduced with the same short piece of rhythmic music, which everybody knew. The achievements of our submarines were also constantly highlighted in the same way through news flashes. When, for instance, we happened to be in the garden, and heard this piece of music playing, everybody would rush to the nearest radio to listen to what had happened. Of course defeats were not announced this way, but in the first years of the war there were mostly stunning victories. They continued during the next two years.

I got very nervous thinking that Germany might win the war before I was old enough to join the army and have a part in our victory. Tragically, I am the perfect example of a brainwashed youth who ignorantly volunteered to fight for the filthy purposes of his government. It was the call to greatness on both the personal and national level, which had me hooked and made me put my life on the line. My poor parents, who did not share my enthusiasm, had to watch with trembling hearts as we rushed to disaster.

We escaped the ravages of war until November 1942 when, one afternoon, my father called my mother to his office. I watched her slip through the door adjoining our home which led to his workplace, (he had another entrance which led to the offices of his administration) and suddenly I heard my mother begin to sob hysterically and immediately knew why. Asche, my older brother who was only 18 years old, had been killed in action in Russia on his third day of combat.

He had been drafted and was no friend of the Nazis. As a schoolboy he had tried to get Protestants and Catholics to work together, since we, as Lutherans, were living in a Catholic environment. His opposition to the Nazis was based on his Christian faith and he was nowhere near as superficial as I was. Still, there was no hesitation on his part when he was drafted into the army.

He was shot in the leg during a nightly patrol close to enemy lines. According to the report by his unit leader, he was alive, but could not be carried back by his comrades for reasons unknown to us. The next morning he was missing, and was reported to have bled to death. My sister Sibylle remained unconvinced about the veracity of the report but we never heard anything else about him.

If somebody died in Germany, one would announce it in the newspaper, listing the next of kin with a reference to the Bible or to whatever the family chose. During the war, it had become customary to print "so-and-so" fell in the battle of "such-and-such" place for the Fuehrer, our people, (Volk) and the fatherland. That, of course, was what the Nazis wanted to see. Asche did not die for Hitler. My parents were adamant that they would say nothing of that kind. They courageously referred to God and eternal life.

THE SOVIET UNION ENTERS THE WAR

On June 22, 1941, German attack divisions crossed the border and entered the Soviet Union. The common perception is that Germany started an unprovoked war of aggression against the Soviet Union. Two German generals, Fieldmarshall Keitel and the four-star general Jodl, were convicted by the Nuremberg War Criminal Tribunal of this crime and hanged. In their defense they had consistently stated that it was a pre-emptive strike (like the one in Iraq, I might add) and that is what it was. The Soviet prosecutor team, as well as the Soviet judges, of course knew that it was so, but incapable of applying truth, they had them hanged anyway. It is true that the German army fired the first shot and invaded Russia. That, however, does not make Germany necessarily an aggressor. The real story is quite different. This attack was not the same type of invasion as nearly all the others, which Hitler had ordered earlier.

The reader must be reminded that Western democracies, under the leadership of Franklin Delano Roosevelt and Winston Churchill, allied themselves with the Soviet Union ruled by Stalin long before Hitler rose to the ranks of mass murderers. Josef Stalin and his predecessor Vladimir Ilyich Lenin murdered about 50 million compatriots before World War II. In Brest-Litovsk, Soviet Russia signed a peace treaty with Germany and her allies in 1918. They made huge concessions, ceded vast areas of territory and withdrew from World War I. Russia must "sacrifice space in order to gain time and consolidate power," Lenin argued. He was head of the Communist world revolution, which included the intention to capture Europe. As I already pointed out earlier, the Communists came very close to conquering Germany from within during the post-WWI years.

Stalin stayed the course planning for conquest long before Hitler took over power in Germany. In a speech before the Central Committee of the All-Union Communist Party in July 1925, he laid out his strategy for the Soviet Union entering the war in Europe. In 1939 the British Ambassador, Sir Stafford Cripps, and the American Ambassador, Laurance F. Steinhardt, warned their respective governments that Stalin planned a war not only in Europe but also in Asia. On May 5, 1941, in a speech at the graduation of the Military Academy, Stalin told the leadership of the Soviet Army that it was time to "abandon defensive tactics and adopt a military policy of attack operations."

At the beginning of 1941, the Chief of the Foreign Armies East Branch of the General Staff of the German Army, Colonel Gehlen, pointed out that the build-up of Soviet troops at their eastern border was enough proof for the offensive intention of the Soviet Union.

On August 19, 1939, the Soviet Polit Bureau decided to stand back and observe as a neutral nation while the European nations fought and destroyed each other. Once that process had reached satisfactory level, it was their intention to attack Germany and conquer the whole of Europe. A report about the decisions of that session was published by the French news agency Havas. Stalin had already reported this plan in 1927 during a session of the Central Committee in Moscow.

Foreign ministers Molotov and von Ribbentrop assembled in Moscow and signed the German-Soviet non-Aggression Alliance on August 23, 1939. The pact also included a secret agreement of how to divide Poland between the two powers. Without that alliance Hitler could not have attacked Poland. Stalin was much cleverer than Hitler. He let Hitler open the hostilities and then collected his half of Polish territory later on without firing a shot. Germany was again labeled as an aggressor, but the Soviet Union, which sat in judgment of the German Nazi leaders in Nuernberg, was just as culpable, passively invading Poland while allowing Hitler to do its dirty work.

Viktor Suvoro, an officer in the Soviet general staff and the military intelligence service GRU who fled to Britain in 1978 ("The Icebreaker"); the Austrian Professor Dr. Ernst Topitsch ("Stalin's War");

the German expert on Russian affairs, Wolfgang Strauss ("Project Barbarossa"); the German professor Joachim Hoffmann ("Stalin's War of Extermination, 1941–1945, Planning, Realization and Documentation"), all proved independent of each other and beyond any doubt that the Soviet Union was preparing to invade Germany. This event was scheduled for July 15, 1941. Hitler beat Stalin to it by three weeks. In his book, "Stalin's War," Topitsch described the Soviet long-term strategy against the West, which first used Hitler as battering ram to crush the West, and then followed up by attacking Germany from behind, and conquering Europe. Suvorov's and Hoffmann's books have been translated into English and are available in the United States.

Suvorov comes to the same conclusion and logically titled his book *The Icebreaker.* The icebreaker was Hitler, whom Stalin used for his own plans for world conquest. The four authors agree, as do Baltic leaders, that Stalin's motives for the Molotov-Ribbentrop Alliance were to make Hitler's military aggressions possible by pretending to give him a free ride. The signing of this alliance marks the real beginning of World War II, wrote Suvorov. Strauss called it the initial ignition for the Soviet war of aggression. From a Soviet standpoint it was a just war since it was supposed to advance the world revolution. According to Suvarov, "On August 23, 1939, Stalin had won World War II before Hitler even started it." Thanks to tremendous resources in manpower and production strength, the Soviet Union was able to recover from original severe beatings and win; Hitler's irrationality only helped. Stalin did not get the whole of Europe, as he had planned, but did secure the Eastern branch. France, the Benelux and some other countries may not like what I say, but like it or not, it was the German Army that saved them from Soviet rule.

Before the war with Germany, the Soviet Union had led wars of aggression against Estonia, Latvia, Lithuania (which they occupied), Poland, Finland and Rumania. They stole part of the territory of those three nations and 24 million people were incorporated into the Soviet totalitarian system. The Soviet concentration camps were overcrowded with prisoners from the occupied territories. The officers of those countries were killed by the thousands.

Russian President Vladimir Putin declared at the 60th anniversary of the end of WWII that "good had won against evil." The former president of Lithuania, Vytauta Landsbergis, saw the issue differently and the presidents of Estonia and Lithuania, Arnold Ruuti and Valdas Adamkus, had rejected an invitation from Putin to participate in the victory celebrations in Moscow. Referring to this rejection, Landsbergis stated in an interview with the German newspaper "Die Welt" the following: "...in Moscow we are supposed to celebrate the liberation of Europe from Nazi Germany by the Red Army. It is however a fact that Russia as the Soviet Union caused this war...Putin wants everybody to understand that the liberation from National Socialism is being celebrated when in fact Russia celebrates its conquests, which are parts of Rumania, Hungary, Slovakia, Finland, East Poland, Koenigsberg, and the Baltic States,—these nations were all attacked by the Soviet Union before Hitler attacked the Soviet Union on June 21, 1941. The invitation to Moscow therefore means, that the enslaved states are supposed to celebrate their own imprisonment."

Putin refused to apologize to the Baltic countries for the aggression, occupation, and consequent suffering of their populations. He pointed out that the Supreme Soviet had declared the Molotov/Ribbentrop pact void in 1989. With that done, according to Putin, the issue had been dealt with and was thus closed. "We don't want to talk about it anymore," he said in an interview with "Die Welt." I am sure that every other criminal would like to force a pardon for his crimes in a similar way. If I didn't know it before, I know it now, Putin is a fake democrat. "Once KGB, always KGB" was the answer a Russian lawyer gave me to my question about what she thought of the Russian president. He is not interested in people and other nations.

Through a detailed examination of Soviet troop movement in the months before the German attack, Suvarov proves from essentially public sources, that the Soviet Union amassed huge armies totaling 198 divisions, in offensive positions ready to attack from the border regions. Similarly, Hoffmann counts 258 divisions and 165 flight regiments.

Hitler had four tank groups while Stalin had 16 attack armies. At the border to Rumania the ninth attack army was only 60 miles away from the oil fields, without which Germany would have broken down. This Soviet army with it seven corps disposing of 3341 tanks on its own posed a deadly threat. The whole German army had just 3550 tanks of which 1700 had only light armor and were no match for the Soviet tanks. Stalin marshaled of a total of 14,000–15,000 tanks. This, however, according to Hoffmann, is a highly conservative estimate. If we count the tanks that were part of the 92 mechanized divisions, as well as the numerous independent armored battalions with their own tanks, one could come to a total figure of 22,000 Soviet tanks.

The relationship of planes, artillery and infantry was similarly disproportionate. Combat-ready German aircraft numbering 2,500 (2,121 according to other sources) faced 10,000 to 15,000 Soviet aircraft. Four hundred two airfields were built close to the border. German artillery pieces numbering 7,145 faced 37,000 Soviet artillery pieces out of the 148,000 cannons and mortars already produced by the Soviet armament industry. The 3.2 million German soldiers faced ca. 13.5 million Soviet soldiers including 10 corps of airborne troops and paratroopers numbering 1 million soldiers, as well as artillery and swim tanks geared toward an offensive. Along the whole border the Soviets eliminated all fortifications and minefields so that their attack divisions were not going to be slowed down by them. Germany did precisely the same.

I know that my father was deeply worried when the war with the Soviet Union started but I was far from it. We ran to the radio nearly every day when March music introduced another report of a stunning victory. There were huge encirclement battles with hundred thousands of prisoners of war taken. Our armies were closing in on Moscow. The reason for such victories was made clear to us only many years after the war—the Soviet divisions were in the middle of moving into attack positions when the German forces struck.

They were not prepared for a defensive type of warfare. A great part of their air force, for instance, which was supposed to carry airborne divisions behind German lines, was of no use in defense causing Soviet frontlines to crumble. We youngsters thought that we were invincible and I grew even more frustrated because it seemed to be obvious that we would win the war before I could get into it.

GODLESSNESS AND SELF-DESTRUCTION

Collections for warm clothes for our soldiers began in the fall of 1941. That winter, an especially frigid season began early and as incredible as it sounds—the army was insufficiently equipped to surmount the cold. Even gloves were lacking in the quantities necessary to enable our troops to stay warm. And then the war began to take another direction.

In my view, there were several important factors that led to putting the German army into a defensive posture. First and foremost, the evil of Nazi philosophy put into action led to its own self-destruction. When Wehrmacht soldiers swiftly advanced into the depths of Russia, special SS units followed right on their heels. The SS units, who in an effort to carry out the Nazi philosophy that Jews, Gypsies, Slavs, and others, were not worth living, rounded them up for extermination. These innocent people were then casually executed without any formality.

Initially German troops were welcomed by the population as liberators from Communist oppression. But as the news of these executions spread, joy dissolved into hatred. Instead of winning allies and helping the people to become masters of their own destiny, Hitler transformed them into embittered enemies. Behind German lines partisans began to operate, fighting the invaders. And in the end, there was no denying the truth that evil destroys those who commit it as well as those who appease it.

In the context of evil I need to mention that not all, who had a chance, died without a fight. In April of 1943, Hitler decided that the inhabitants of the Warsaw ghetto were to be liquidated and charged Heinrich Himmler, his top SS leader, with the execution of the order. SS troops encircled the ghetto. Male Jews had taken position inside of it. On April 21 the uprising started and fierce fighting followed until the German air force was called in to bomb the ghetto, which was completely destroyed. Twelve thousand Jews died. They knew that they could neither escape nor survive but they didn't want to be slaughtered like lambs and instead, fought like lions.

There were uprisings in concentration camps as well, one in Treblinca on August 2, 1943. From roughly 1000 inmates, 70 to 80 were able to escape. On October 14 of the same year 300 Jews fled from Sobibor though a mere 47 survived the ordeal. There may be others I am unaware of.

Another factor for our defeat involved a standing order issued by Hitler himself. It stated that German soldiers must never give up conquered territory. That became fatal a year later, when a German army of 250,000 soldiers was encircled in Stalingrad by Soviet forces. When General Friedrich Paulus, the commander of the Stalingrad army, realized that he was in a no-win situation, he asked his superior officer and commander of the Southern section of German forces in the Soviet Union, Fieldmarschall Erich von Manstein, for permission to break out and lead his army back to the German front lines.

At that stage of the conflict it would have been possible to do it but Manstein was afraid to disobey Hitler's order and covered his back by telling Paulus that he would give him every help he needed in case he decided to break out. These two officers tried to get the other one to shoulder the responsibility for disobeying Hitler. They knew that the order was strategic nonsense and would be fatal for the encircled army, but neither dared to challenge it. They hid behind formality because they were afraid for their positions and reputations. Ultimately, the Stalingrad army was destroyed, with 250,000 soldiers either killed or captured. And capture by the Soviets was not much different than falling in battle anyway for it boiled down to those who refused to cooperate being killed. The Stalingrad defeat was the turning point of the war.

My Military Service

I entered into military service in July 1943 conscripted as an officer aspirant into the reserve and training unit of the elite army division "Grossdeutschland" (Great-Germany) in Guben in the Lausitz. I had originally wanted to become a fighter pilot, but I didn't pass the test because I was said to be colorblind. Therefore I chose artillery instead, which was the branch my grandfather and father both served as officers in WWI.

When I got to Guben, I was given the choice of the type of artillery I desired. I went with assault artillery because I believed it to be the most exciting branch of the weaponry. The vehicle was in reality a tank without a turning tower. Our task was to accompany the infantry during an attack, frighten and eliminate the resistance of enemy strongholds. We had to aim by turning the whole tank towards our target. We also had less armor at the top of the vehicle, since the vehicle was designed to support an offensive and not operate behind enemy lines.

After a grueling year of hard-hitting basic training, I was promoted to sergeant. As I said earlier, no ideological instruction existed in the military so I did not have to answer for my beliefs, only my capability in combat counted. The biggest highlight of the time was the monthly food parcels sent by my mother. Stuffed with everything I liked, I don't remember how many men were in our sleeping quarters, but every one of them waited for this parcel as anxiously as I did because I always shared the goodies with my fellow soldiers.

In July of 1944 I was transferred to assault artillery brigade 191. Our theatre of combat would be Yugoslavia (facing the Red Army). We went down to Nish in the South of Serbia with all our equipment on our own special train. The journey lasted two weeks. It was during this journey that we learned from the news over the radio about Count Stauffenberg's attempt to kill Hitler on July 20, 1944. I remember this broadcast very well because the radio anchorman read a list of names of conspirators linked to Stauffenberg. There were many well-known names of top German families, including Field Marshall Erwin von Witzleben. The ferocious attacks on the characters of those named in that list sounded shallow to me, and deep inside I quietly thought what a pity it was that the attempt had failed. Once in Yugoslavia we were not provided with daily news and the matter faded away.

We normally were housed in private quarters and often lodged with German families. Sometimes we would go into combat and return to the same quarters, other times we were assigned to different accommodations. Wherever we made our beds, compared to infantry soldiers who had to stay out in the field, we led a much better life. It included plenty of time to rest in exceptional living quarters.

Most of our action involved the support of retreating infantrymen. Memorable were the days of fierce street fights in Belgrade, a fearful prospect because we were shot at from high buildings and our armor on the top was not the best. I was the gunner and had to shoot at the targets given to me relying on the commandant who tried to advise me of the distance.

After the battle for Belgrade, I remember, we were positioned on a river with the Soviets encamped on the other side. Among their forces was a battalion of women soldiers who had a well-earned reputation for being very cruel, so we didn't want to fall into their hands. While we were camped there, I engaged and sank two Soviet gunboats, which was really business as usual and not a big deal. Nonetheless, I was awarded the Iron Cross for my prowess in combat.

At the end of March 1945, I was sent to an officer's academy in

Germany and had to walk some distance to the railway station to catch a train to get there. Still located in Yugoslavia, suddenly I noticed the disturbing drone of an aircraft which turned out to be a four-engine American bomber. It was my only encounter with American forces. The bomber seemed to come after me as I ran as fast as I could until I jumped behind a wall for cover. As I did, the plane's machine guns began to strafe an anti-aircraft artillery position near my hiding place. Thankfully I escaped injury and was able to continue my journey.

When I finally arrived in Guben that April, it turned out that the officer's academy had been shut down. In retrospect, I should have never left my unit in the first place because the Soviet and allied forces were already in Germany and close to meeting each other. I was now in danger of being picked up by any unit that might be organized on the spot and thrown into battle which was the last thing I wanted. I managed to get myself a marching order to return to my unit and got on the next train that went toward Vienna and Yugoslavia.

It was but a few weeks before Germany's final collapse and yet with all I had seen, it was still inconceivable that we would lose the war. There had been considerable talk of the "miracle weapons" which we all expected would now be brought forward and change the destiny of our nation. The miracle weapons we expected were supposed to be missiles, rockets, or some other type of superior firepower. It didn't speak well of my intelligence to believe these stories and as it turned out I might as well have believed in the Easter Bunny.

I finally reached my unit and it was shortly thereafter that the end of the war reached us.

My brother Burchard was drafted into the army in April 1945 at age 17. He then became part of a brigade which operated east of the river Elbe in retreat from the approaching Red Army. Burchard and his unit managed to cross the Elbe. They became American prisoners of war, a status he did not retain very long. A short time after his capture he fell from a truck, broke an arm, and was released immediately with very little formality.

RESISTANCE TO HITLER

There was a steady resistance mounted against the Nazi regime from the get-go. Initially it came from the Social Democrats and Communists but most of them were known and therefore they didn't pose a real threat for the government. I do not count the Communists as true part of the resistance—they were competitors for totalitarian power with a similar evil philosophy.

There were quite a number of unconnected groups and individuals who fought the Nazis but had never a chance within the police state to unseat Hitler. The only group that had the organization to achieve it was the military whose efforts culminated in Count Klaus von Stauffenberg's failed attempt to kill Hitler on July 20, 1944.

In the context of this book, I shall concentrate and tell only the stories of Dietrich Bonhoeffer, Hans and Sophie Scholl, and Count von Stauffenberg. The story of the resistance is a story of innumerable individuals, men and women, old and young, rich and poor, who put their lives, reputations, and fortunes on the line to try and prevent evil from seizing the soul and destiny of Germany. Those whom I write about here paid with their lives to follow the dictates of their conscience. God comes before government.

HANS AND SOPHIE SCHOLL, DIETRICH BONHOEFFER

Hans and Sophie Scholl founded an organization called "The White Rose" (Die Weisse Rose) while students at the Munich University. They chose that name because it expressed their passion to speak the unwavering truth with purity. "We are not silent. We are your conscience. We shall not leave you in peace," they told the German people. Accompanying the Scholls were Willi Graf, Kurt Huber, Christoph Probst, and Alexander Schmorell. Huber was the only professor among them and he had great influence on the students. All of them rejected the totalitarian nature of the regime, the arbitrary arrests, the concentration camps, and the war. They defended the values important to them—freedom, love of neighbor, love of life, and faith in God.

Their first leaflets appeared in 1942 and at that time Sophie didn't realize that her brother Hans was the driving force behind the action. She eventually joined him and in subsequent leaflets they called for resistance against National Socialism, attacked the lies of the Nazi establishment, and decried the mass murder of Jews.

In addition, they proclaimed the responsibility of each German to do something about it. Recognizing that the war could not be won, they called for passive resistance and sabotage. In February of 1943 they wrote the slogans "Down with Hitler," "Freedom," and "Hitler the Mass Murderer" on the walls of the inner city of Munich.

On the 18th of that same month Hans and Sophie Scholl were arrested. On February 22 they appeared in court and were sentenced to death by Roland Freisler, president of the "People's Court," a well-known Nazi of the lowest category who had them executed the same day by guillotine. Shortly afterwards the other three students were arrested and executed as well. More people in other parts of Germany who were connected with them were also arrested. In Hamburg alone, 50 people were arrested and sentenced to prison terms, while eight were executed.

"There is only one choice for us," they stated in their leaflets, "that each one of us fights for our future, our freedom, our honor in a state that is conscious of its moral responsibility. Freedom and honor! The German name will be forever discredited if not the German youth rises, avenges and at the same time atones for those crimes and smashes its torturers and creates a new and spiritual Europe. The German people look to us. Our nation begins to rise against the enslavement of Europe through National Socialism, in a new breakthrough of freedom and honor."

Bonhoeffer is well known in America. He was a Lutheran pastor and theologian who skillfully articulated his beliefs in both German, and English. A brilliant young man, he was just 21 years old when he was awarded his doctorate with honors. Following that, he spent one year in New York and traveled to Mexico and Cuba. In 1931 Bonhoeffer became youth secretary of the World Alliance for Promoting International Friendship and a member of the Universal Christian Council for Life and Work. From 1933 until 1935 he assumed the pastorate of the German Evangelical Church, Sydenham, and the Reformed Church of St. Paul in London. In Germany he assumed the leadership of the Confessing Church's seminary in the North of the country.

Bonhoeffer returned to New York in 1939 but departed to Germany after just a few weeks. Once back home his insight told him which way the winds of change were blowing and he declared, "Christians face the terrible alternative of willing the defeat of their nation in order that civilization may survive, or willing the victory of their nation and thereby destroying civilization. I know which of these alternatives I must choose."

Bonhoeffer opposed the Nazi regime on biblical grounds, and had been close to the resistance circle around Admiral Wilhelm Canaris, head of the German Military Counter Intelligence since 1938. Daringly he advocated publicly on behalf of the Jews and courageously helped a group of them to escape to Switzerland. Unique in his understanding of the organic interaction between religion, politics, and culture, Bonhoeffer had originally been a pacifist. However, he changed his position so dramatically that his work with the military resistance included helping plan an attempt to assassinate Hitler.

"Will the church merely gather up those whom the wheel has crushed," he argued, "or will we prevent the wheel from crushing them?" His sister-in law quoted him with this reasoning: "If I see a madman driving a car into a group of innocent bystanders, then I can't, as a Christian, simply wait for the catastrophe to happen, then comfort the wounded and bury the dead. I must try to wrestle the steering wheel out of the hands of the driver."

"It is one of the most astonishing and at the same time most irrefutable experiences," he once stated, "that evil—often in a surprisingly short space of time—proves stupid and ineffectual. This does not mean that each individual misdeed is often immediately punished, but it demonstrates the fact that disregard, as a matter of principle, of the divine Commandments in the supposed interests of self-preservation, often has the contrary effect. It seems to emerge with certainty from this that there are laws in human society that are stronger than all forces, which try to raise themselves above them; it is therefore not only unjust but also stupid to spurn those laws."

Dietrich Bonhoeffer was arrested and imprisoned in the spring of 1943 because of his involvement in helping Jews to escape; his connections to the resistance were discovered later. He was hanged in the concentration camp at Flossenbrueg on April 9, 1945, and was one of four of his immediate family to be executed by the Nazi regime.

THE JULY 20, 1944, COUP D'ETAT

The July 20, 1944, attempt to kill Hitler by Colonel Count Claust von Stauffenberg was by no means the first one. Stauffenberg had come close to several other attempts that same year, which had to be aborted for various reasons. Measures to take Hitler out of power by the military began as early as 1938, when a number of high-ranking officers realized that the Fuehrer was taking Germany into war. Another attempt was undertaken by General Henning von Treskow who placed a bomb in Hitler's plane in 1943. Unfortunately, the ignition failed.

In addition to attempts on Hitler's life, detailed plans to arrest Hitler were also made in 1938. Erwin von Witzleben, later on Field Marshall, the commander of Berlin, Count Walter von Brockdorff-Ahlefeldt, commander of Potzdam garrison, and General-Colonel Erich Hoepner, commander of a tank division, were the leaders of the intended action.

But the plans included more than military personnel. Through the State Secretary in the Foreign Office, Ernst von Weizsaecker, Dr. Theo von Kordt, second in command in the German embassy in London, was charged with contacting the British foreign secretary Lord Halifax, to keep him apprised of developments in Germany under Hitler. Sadly, instead of listening to him, then British Prime Minister Neville Chaimberlain traveled to Munich to meet with Hitler and the French and Italian leaders. The result was that Hitler gained possession of the Sudetenland, and the allies were duped into thinking they got peace; the conspirators lost the momentum and had no foreign backing. It was not the right time for a coup against a popular Hitler.

Not long afterwards the German resistance made several attempts to contact the British government. In the summer of 1939, Count Gerhard von Schwerin, head of the department of England/America in the General Staff of the Army, went to London to convince the British government to send a squadron of warships to Danzig. Others, including the head of the German military counter intelligence, Admiral Wilhelm Canaris, tried the same later. Canaris informed the British of high-level military secrets and warned them of the looming invasion of The Netherlands and France.

Prime Minister Churchill and Foreign Minister Eden refused to take the German resistance seriously. They erroneously defined their efforts as an in-house battle of one Nazi group against another Nazi group. Speaking in the British Parliament August 2, 1944, Churchill declared that the attempt to kill Hitler was part of "liquidation battles between dignitaries of the Third Reich." A week later the New York Times wrote that the assassination attempt reminds more of the "evil atmosphere of the underworld" than one, which is expected "normally in the officer corps of a civilized nation." This is the same newspaper that described Fidel Castro as a land reformer in 1950.

It was then decided within the resistance that to kill Hitler was the only way to release the leaders of the armed forces from their oath. The issue of trying to take the life of the head of state who everybody had sworn an oath of allegiance to was a central issue. Stauffenberg stated, "It is time to do something now. Anyone, however, who dares to do something, must be aware, that most likely he will enter history as a traitor. In case he would abstain from action, then he would be a traitor to his conscience. I could not look into the eyes of the wives and children of our fallen, if I didn't try to do everything possible to prevent the sacrifice of human lives."

The explosion of the bomb which Stauffenberg planted close to Hitler in his headquarters on July 20, 1944, did not kill him, but instead left only superficial scratches. The military uprising collapsed as 1500 people were arrested and 200 of them were executed. They were patriots and belonged to the crème of German society. Among them were 19 Generals, 26 Colonels, 2 Ambassadors, 7 diplomats, 1 cabinet member, 3 state-secretaries, the head of the German criminal investigation, and many high-ranking civil servants.

Millions more people died as Germany continued down its path of total destruction.

CHAPTER FIVE

THE BOMBING

THE FIVE YEARS of bombardment suffered by German cities and villages is without parallel in world history. In addition to the expulsion and flight of the entire population of the Eastern provinces of the country as well as other Eastern European countries, it was the biggest catastrophe on German soil since the Thirty-Years-War in the 17th century. More than a thousand cities and villages were mercilessly pounded. One million tons of high explosives and firebombs fell upon 30 million civilians, mostly women, children, and old people. More than half a million of them died. The loss of urban landscape, grown over centuries, was irretrievable.

Dresden and Hamburg remain as well known historical symbols of these years of destruction. But the sweeping scope of this devastation was revealed just recently 60 years later. In the beginning only high-explosive bombs which did not destroy a city all at once were used. Koeln was bombed 262 times, Essen 262 times, Duesseldorf 243 times, and Duisberg 299 times. In the last four months of the war the allied bombers dropped 370,000 tons of explosives on German cities. The city of Dresden, which was crammed with refugees from the Eastern provinces, was destroyed with 650,000 firebombs and 1,474 tons of high-explosive bombs. The attack was completed the next morning with 800 allied bombers and fighter planes firing their machine guns on fleeing civilian survivors.

Air Vice-Marshall Arthur Harris with the nickname 'Bomber Harris' was in charge of the British air fleets. He had served before in various countries including in the Middle East, where he led the 58th Squadron at the end of the twenties. In those years the RAF used terror bombing, including gas attacks and delayed action bombs, on the Iraqi tribes rebelling against British rule. With regards to the bombing of Germany his biographer stated that all decisions had been made conjointly, "Churchill had insisted emphatically, that one German city after the other was to be destroyed."

He fathered the concept when he was cabinet minister of armament in WWI planning an attack of 1000 bombers on Berlin. The assault didn't take place because the war ended before the aircraft could be built and idea executed. "The battle of 1919 was not fought," he wrote in 1925, "but the ideas remained alive...For the first time a group of civilized people have the possibility to condemn the other group to complete helplessness...Perhaps the next time the issue will be to kill women and children and the civilian population in general." And that is what we have today!

In 1943 the specialists discovered that it is easier to burn down a city than to destroy it with high-explosive bombs. The destructive capacity of fire bombs gradually increased as the effectiveness of their use was analyzed. Sophisticated designs were produced to maximize the destruction of buildings and the number of people who could be killed.

The bishop of Chichester, Dr. George Bell, told the British House of Lords on February 11, 1943, that "To equalize the Nazi murderers with the German people means to advance barbarism." In February of 1944 he attacked the evil of the bombing. Conversely, Professor Freeman Dyson, a physician in the Operational Research Center of the Bomber Command, wrote in 1984, "I felt sick from what I knew. Many times I decided that I have the moral obligation to run to the street and tell the British people about the stupidities that are being done in their name. But I didn't have the courage to do it. Until the end I sat in my office and calculated how to murder another 100,000 people in the most economic way possible."

At no time did our family have to suffer from the bombing. Freiwaldau and the Sudetenland remained an island of peace—from the war and from the Nazis. We, however, were hit only at the very end of the war, but it was an equally devastating blow.

CHAPTER SIX

THE END OF THE WAR

THE SUFFERING OF MY FATHER

ON MAY 10, 1945, my parents stood behind the curtains of our apartment in Freiwaldau and watched the Soviet troops filter into our city. My father, the highest-ranking civil servant in the city and area, could have left the city a few days earlier just as the top Nazi functionary had already done. It was unthinkable for him to flee and leave behind the people he governed when they could not do the same. He was a public servant in the true sense of the word. Since he had saved a number of Jews and Czechs from persecution by the Nazi machinery, he was not preoccupied with what might happen to him. He should have fled because there was nothing more he could have done for others.

There was a knock at the door a few moments after watching the troops occupy our city and Soviet soldiers took my father away. My mother brought him clothing and food the next day and realized as they looked at each other, that he thought this would be the last time that they would ever see one another in this world. He was right.

For two weeks my mother stayed alone in our home. One day a colonel of the Red Army came by and asked to see my father's clothing. When my mother showed it to him he selected the best he could find. She drew his attention to the fact that her husband was much taller than he and therefore the suits he was taking would not fit him. He smiled and said that "tailors make everything new."

Without warning, one day my mother was told to leave her home within minutes. She was allowed to take only what she could carry, which wasn't very much. Nervously she collected a number of things, and then she was taken to the railway station, put on a coal train, and that was the last she ever saw of Freiwaldau.

She went to pick up my sister Sibylle in Thueringen, which was in the Soviet occupation zone, and both crossed over to the British occupation zone in the back of a British army truck on its way west from Berlin. Seven years later my mother received the following letter from the former mayor of Freiwaldau; he had been taken away together with my father. My father had done nothing wrong and committed no crime, nor did the writer of the following letter.

Kempten/Allgäu, April 2, 1952

My Dear Lady!

I was given your address some six weeks ago, but my letter has remained unwritten until today. As far as I am concerned, writing this letter was more than just a matter of honour. It was also a heartfelt need. Be that as it may, until now I did not feel mentally prepared to do so. When I received your dear letter last Monday through Mrs Grete Nebauer, for which I am most grateful, I knew that I could now delay no longer. I have already read your letter four times and will probably read it several times more. All those vanished recollections are appearing again before my very eyes. I see the days of October 1938 and everything then unfurls like a reel of film—I see everything in my mind's eye, hundreds of memorable hours in which one man always played the leading role, a man whom I came to love and honour, with a character and a heart full of goodness and love, your husband, our Landrat.

My dear lady, you want to have a report which tells the truth, you want to follow in his footsteps with your children. I will tell the story to you to the best of my ability, as far as I am able to recollect all these hours. I want to try to explain things exactly as they happened, but I know too that I am unable to convey just what was going on at that time in your husband's heart and mind. I cannot do so because it would be beyond the power of mere words to tell it as it really was. I only know that your husband stood his terrible suffering patiently with an insatiable longing for you and his children burning in his heart, a longing which surpassed everything, yes everything else. I recognized that longing time and time again from the deep, deep sighs which emerged from his innermost being when his brown eyes looked at me, when he sought my hand and saw in me the only person who understood him and was willing to give comfort, without a word passing between us.

My dear lady, the relationship between us was not that between a county commissioner and a mayor but between two tormented and martyred creatures who realized full well that the people around us had their own troubles and were not even willing to say a kind word to their neighbours. That realization brought us still closer together and so we spent most of the hours of the day, hand in hand, in close contact with one another. But, my dear lady, I want to give you some idea of all that he suffered during these days and how he did so! We realized that we shared a common destiny and we became brothers. If it can be of any small consolation to you, dear lady and to your dear children, I tried to the very best of my ability to relieve your husband's suffering, however, slightly, if only by laying my coat and blanket over his wounded body or placing his head in my lap so that the terrible feeling of being abandoned without any comrade close to hand was somewhat alleviated. Throughout his life your husband always stood his ground in every situation but in face of this unspeakable suffering, this need and torment, he had become a helpless child, so completely powerless that I will bear the elevated feeling in my heart for the rest of my life that I was a friend to a rare and noble man until the final hour of his existence.

May God be my witness that I am not writing a single word which is not the purest truth, I must tell it to you so that you and your children will at least know, when you think back on him, that he was not totally abandoned. In quieter hours, he recounted his whole life to me; he described the days of his young love, the happiness when Asche was born, everything—yes, everything. Perhaps, throughout the life that you shared, your husband did not speak those words which he spoke to me, words of happiness and supreme satisfaction with the partner in his life and with his children whom he loved from the depths of his soul and with all his heart. Despite all his suffering and the expectation of a terrible end, he thought only of you and your children, and he prayed that God might protect you all—believe me, all this is true, I alone know the truth and can tell you that his last thoughts were with you.

When we set out from Freiwaldau on Ascension Day in 1945, our next stop was in Friedberg, where we spent the night in a classroom in the local vocational school, the Steinfach-schule. The other classrooms were occupied by enemy soldiers. Early in the morning in the courtyard we were shown a Russian soldier who had been severely beaten up. Municipal Chief Inspector Hauke, who had learned a little Russian in the First World War, heard that we would suffer the same fate. But nothing happened here. We were even given some warm tinned food to eat and then we were taken away in a closed truck with no windows and under close guard to Bad Landeck.

We were put up in the cellar of a spa building and counted five or six times during the night. That night, Hauke was taken away for a cross-examination; he was away for a long time and gave no detailed answer to our questions. A little later it was your husband's turn to be examined but his questioning was very short and one thing they asked him was whether he had been a member of the SS. He tried to explain and tell them to which part of the army he really belonged. The interpreter was an Indian who grinned and said that they knew everything. In the morning the three of us, your husband, Hauke and I, were taken by car to Glatz and locked up there in the fortress cells. Our names were called out repeatedly during the night and they said we were going to be shot. In fact, there was incessant machine gun firing outside, the shots went on without interruption. Then the morning came and things quietened down. All we were given to eat that day was a bowl of soup but your husband did not eat a single spoonful, despite our efforts to persuade him. Otherwise things were quiet. At night it began all over again, the first cross-examinations took place and they were merciless. We lay on the floor as though dead. The next morning we were taken to a prison and there too we witnessed terrible moments, in the night we dug our own graves but once again it turned out that these graves were for others.

About four days later, we came to a different prison in a cellar measuring about 30 square meters with a little window right up at the top of the ceiling. When the door was opened, there were at least 45 persons inside, some squatting and others standing; we could scarcely get our feet inside and stood there with our few possessions under our arm when they closed the door again and we heard the key turn. I will never forget those sounds, the key in the lock, the door thrown open, the guard counting the prisoners, itself an indescribable act; when he got to six, the first attempt already failed and he had to start again and it took an incredibly long time until the guard left again, without being really convinced that nobody was missing. Half an hour later the same maneuver was repeated by another soldier, then they closed the door again and hardly had the key been taken away than the huge bunch of keys could be heard again and we saw an eye staring in through the spy hole; then it went away again, only for the door to be thrown open suddenly and a name called out, almost impossible to understand; the man was let out and sometimes he came back later, sometimes he did not. And so it went on minute after minute, the guards with their guns stamping their feet outside, the rattle of the bunch of keys, the key pushed into the lock and taken away again without opening the door, the eye shining behind the spy hole, counting the prisoners yet again; boots stamped on people or on their limbs, but we dared not make any sign of complaint, we must not make any sound of pain or attract anyone's attention. A bitter revenge was exacted on anyone who dared to do so. An hour has 60 minutes, and a day, just one day, 24 hours. Day and night we knew no rest, no peace, we were watched all the time; the sensation of fear never left us, and all the time the horrible stench of the people whose bodily needs were performed on chamber pots that were far too small and emptied only in the early morning and evening. All night long the light shone brightly and we waited for our only meal, an indefinable soup—all this turned our lives into an unspeakable torment.

In this cellar, there were nine Germans and the other 35 or so were Russian soldiers, all of them from Mongolia. Only a few hours passed before I felt the first lice bite. We tried to find a little corner where we could squat because lying down was entirely out of the question, we could only sit with our legs drawn close up to our stomachs and after a time you had to stand up again but then you were obliged to return to your previous position to prevent your neighbour from spreading his own space to gain a more comfortable posture; it was a helpless situation which made our lives an extreme misery in the truest sense of the term. In this hell hole, your husband did not have to suffer any further maltreatment but I was taken outside for some little time between early in the morning and late at night, and I can still hear the words that your husband spoke softly when I was pushed back in again, "My God, my God." Sometimes a human life is over in an instant and I still do not really know just how much horror a man can take. Because of the conditions in this hellhole, after just a few days we looked very, very bad, there was no air and no food, we could not wash and were unshaven, we could not see ourselves but we could gain some idea by looking at the appearance of our other comrades. And behind it all, the constant fear. When we were driven out into the prison yard on 1 June, we could see practically nothing at all, our entire bodies were bruised by the stone floor, our eyes were blinded by the sunlight and many of us collapsed. I supported your husband because he seemed about to fall over. Suddenly other people turned up, including the entire police force from the town and my comrades who had been taken away with us from Freiwaldau but had been held until now in Landeck. It took them a long time to realize who we were. Your husband looked so terrible that he was truly impossible to recognize.

We were loaded on to a truck, so many of us that sitting on the floor we had to put out forearms over the legs of the next man. We were jammed in on the floor in 3 rows from front to back so that we could quite literally not move a hand. I will never forget this journey in all my life. Under heavy guard, we set out very early in the morning and as we were passing a church I heard the bell strike. Nobody knew where we were going. Only Germans were in the truck and most of them came from the Reich. There were frequent long halts on the very bad roads, because war damage had made the streets impassable or bridges had been blown up and we often had to go back the way we had come. Sometimes we thought the truck would keel over and that would surely have been the best thing that God could have done for us. I simply cannot describe what we had to put up with that morning. Our bruised bodies, the bone shaking truck, not able for a second to move even the smallest part of our body, no appeals for mercy were listened to and nobody was allowed to get down to perform their bodily needs, above us the burning sun, and an intolerable thirst; all this went on without interruption until 5 in the afternoon when we drove in to the prison yard in Oppeln.

Nobody could get down because all our limbs were rigid and some of us had seen them die off quite literally. So we were rolled down like dogs, received with kicks on the ground and two men were already dead. Nobody had noticed their death, I believe that I cannot describe our suffering because after seven years I myself can scarcely believe that that anybody could suffer so much and really experience all this.

The guards who received us here were all young men, one red-haired sergeant roared at us to stand up. I believe that your husband was almost fainting when this fox-red beast kicked him in the groin and genitals so hard that he yelled out. I tried to help the big man to stand up and dragged him in to the prison where the others were already standing. The two dead bodies lay outside. We had to undress completely, turn out the pockets of our clothing and everything was taken away from us. Then we and our clothing were taken for delousing, our hair was cut and we were taken back into cellars where we collapsed on the stone floor with no bedding of any kind. Then the first meal of the day came, it was a cabbage soup with sauerkraut boiled in water, but we greedily ate this horror despite all the dirt on the tin cans in which it was handed to us. Then our names were written down and your husband and I were allocated to the police with the word "Sibinsky."

We did not care any longer because all this could not possibly continue for long.

On the following days cabbage soup was served to us three times and the result was of course that everyone suffered from terrible diarrhoea. The chamber pots were nowhere near sufficient, they overflowed and were only emptied in the early morning and evening. One morning we were taken out into the yard where we were able to go to the toilet. Planks had been laid across a hole in the ground and hundreds of men, women and young girls ran like people possessed to these boards. Men pulled down their trousers, women raised their skirts and we emptied our bowels with a terrible outpouring only to see thousands of flies alighting on our naked bodies, women shouted out, men collapsed in to the muck—and when we were back in our hellhole of a prison I spoke to your husband about what we had just experienced and he said that nobody would believe what we had seen. And so it went on day after day. The stench in the cell was intolerable.

On 10 June, we received the first medical attention, first from a field orderly and then a lady doctor. We scraped the charcoal off burned lumps of wood but all we were given to eat was cabbage soup, nothing but cabbage soup. On 15 June the three of us—your husband, Hauck and I, with some others, were sent to the rest room at the top of the prison where there were 24 of us and I felt the blood running down my legs. Up there we were not given any more cabbage soup but a little of some other slimy brew and drops every day. One or two of us died every day and 12 to 15 were carted off to the cemetery. And so it went on, day after day.

One man from Berlin was able to speak Russian and he worked as a nursing orderly. I asked him to give me some drops which Red Cross Sister Ruth—I do not remember her other name, her father was employed in the provincial council office and they came from Zuckmantel and she was working in a foreign hospital—always stole for your husband because she was assisting the Russian doctors. My sister-in-law has just remembered the name of the Red Cross sister: she was called Ruth Kosma! She had been dragged away with Dr. Moser and also taken to Oppeln. Your husband was doing rather better now. I too, was able to go to see Ruth every day to have my wound bandaged and received heart drops from the lady doctor at Ruth's request for your husband and me. On 2 July, your husband also went down with me and was able to speak to Ruth for a few minutes and she told us that she was to be released on 3 July. Your husband sent his greetings with her to you, dear lady. As I later found out she only got as far as Freiwaldau, God only knows into whose hands she fell.

On 4 July your husband's health deteriorated again, he fainted several times, and I asked the nursing attendant to call the doctor who came along and put your husband in a cell next to her treatment room. On 5 July I went to have my bandages changed and asked for permission to visit my comrade because today was his birthday. The doctor refused to begin with but then let me go to see him. My hopes remained unfulfilled—when we kissed goodbye, I knew that this was our final goodbye. On 6 July, he went to the toilet opposite, where he collapsed and died a few moments later, as the lady doctor told me after looking after my bandages. He lay there in the corridor—the tears filled my eyes and I could not see—but I think his eyes were closed. He was already cold. Yesterday I remembered his last words: "Karl, if you ever survive, go and see my wife and tell her that I send my greetings to her and to our children and pray that God may protect them." When I asked to be allowed to accompany his body to the cemetery, the blows rained down on my body. The leader of the local farmers in Hannsdorf, in the district of Glatz—whose name I have forgotten—was out there too. Your husband, the county Commissioner, is lying with two other comrades, whose names I do not know, in a grave, naked, in the cemetery near Oppeln, I no longer remember the name of the place near the River Oder. But I will find it again if the time to do so ever comes. A few lines have been scratched into the stone wall above his grave. I am sure that this place can be found again. After all, there are not hundreds of people buried there, just seven or eight in a single grave.

That was how your husband, the father of your children, met his end, dear lady. He suffered so much, so very much, far more than any human being can imagine, he suffered in his heart and soul. But God will surely be more merciful than men. My dear and honoured lady that is the report which I felt obliged to give you but was afraid to write. These lines are intended only for you and your children. As long as the Eastern powers prevail in Berlin and Vienna and may even one day cross the Rhine, we cannot say a word about things which have happened; the system has woven a net of spies across the whole world reaching out to the smallest village and every word is a terrible risk. I tell you this in deep concern for you and your children because the way in which people are being exterminated is totally unscrupulous. Nobody anywhere is safe against this hatred. You will understand me.

Karl Bittmann
Former Mayor of Freiwaldau

THE FATE OF THE 3.5 MILLION SUDETEN-GERMANS

Author Heinz Nawratil describes how "a German-Slovakian Jew named Mueller died in the infamous 'Theresienstadt' Concentration Camp in Bohemia. He died a quiet, ordinary camp death brought about by hunger, lack of medical care, and constant maltreatment. He perished there at the end of 1945 and his murderers were Czechs, not Germans. The only thing besides the inmates and the administration that was changed at the end of the war were the food rations—they were cut in half. After Mueller the Jew had survived persecution by the Germans, the Czechs finished off Mueller the German. In Czechoslovakia alone after the end of the war there were 1,215 internment camps, 846 labor and prison camps and 215 prisons in which 350,000 Germans were held."

Of the 3.5 million German civilians 270,000 were killed, the rest were expelled just as my mother. Without any historical claim to the German territories, hundreds of thousands of Czechs appropriated the property of the expelled Germans, including our own, moved into the empty houses, and declared themselves the new owners. Years later, after the Iron Curtain was torn down, my brother, sister, brother in law and I, drove by car to Freiwaldau. As we went, we saw decaying houses in villages that did not exist anymore. They were flanked by the remains of forests and vacant areas left by the 700,000 Czechs who lived where 3.5 million Germans used to live; a monument to the stupidity of hatred.

We returned to Freiwaldau to look for our family silver, which my mother and Burchard had buried in a box in our garden a few weeks before the end of the war. Thousands of others had done the same thing but unfortunately, the garden was not there anymore and instead a hospital had been built where our food had once grown. However, the reconstructed landscape was deceptive and we discovered that the silver had been hidden beneath what was now a narrow street. Our metal detector went off but not because of our silver, which somebody else must have found, instead, it responded to the underground metal tubing that serviced the hospital.

The Benesh decrees, an official declaration of the Czechoslovakian government inspired by President Benesh, had justified and legalized the murder of Germans. Navratil catalogs the manner in which Germans were put to death: beating, asphyxiation, stabbing, castration, trampling to death by human beings or horses, burning-alive, mutilation in various ways, pumping full of dung, and rolling to death in barrels.

In Aussig, for instance, 2000 Germans, men, women and children were herded in the streets, beaten to death, thrown into the river Elbe and washed away. And so it was everywhere. These killings were not a series of individual or spontaneous acts of revenge, but rather organized and instigated murders designed to conquer German areas and properties.

To this day, I remain in touch with my former classmates and have not found one of them who wanted revenge. Every person had accepted the loss of their possessions and only wanted justice. The Czech government has to call a spade a spade.

The Red Army Loots, Rapes, Kills, and Burns Down Whole Villages in the East German Provinces

The Atlantic Charter of August 1941 states that "The undersigned countries seek no territorial changes, which do not accord with the freely expressed wishes of the people concerned." Following the tradition established in the Versailles Treaty of not applying one's own principles, Churchill informed the British House of Commons on February 11, 1943 that the Atlantic Charter would not apply to Germany, and that transfers of territories were therefore permissible. At the Yalta Conference in 1944, Roosevelt and Churchill, the Leaders of the Western Alliance, and Stalin further agreed that the German population in East Germany and Eastern Europe had to be expelled. Stalin suggested the summary execution of 50,000 German officers. He had done this to his own officer corps, as well as to 15,000 Polish officers. Churchill answered that 49,999 German officers would be enough.

As a matter of fact, the allied Western forces stopped their advance through Germany by order of their commander General Dwight Eisenhower so that the Red Army could conquer Berlin and occupy a bigger piece of Germany. My sister, Sibylle, was liberated from the Nazis by American soldiers in the province of Thueringen. Shortly thereafter the province was handed over to the totalitarian Soviet system under mass murderer Stalin by Eisenhower.

Because she experienced both up-close-and-personal, Sibylle was qualified to compare the character and conduct of the American soldiers with that of the Soviets. She was working on a farm that cooked daily for 600 French ex-prisoners of war without compensation to serve people in need. When the American soldiers came and asked for food, she found them to be friendly, compassionate, and interested in the fate of the German people they met.

I have noticed American soldiers in Iraq have this same deeply human quality when profiled on Fox News. They share, play with the children, and try to help people in need in addition to risking their lives in combat. America can be proud of their servicemen.

According to Sibylle, Soviet soldiers were quite different. When they came for food it was requisitioned and three of the four women on the farm locked themselves in their rooms, (as all did at night), and only one served the Russians. The house stunk terribly, but thankfully, the women were not raped even though there were no German men around.

One day my mother arrived and she and Sibylle decided to leave for the West. Crossing the demarcation line between the Soviet and the American zones was a daunting hurdle because there were swarms of refugees trying to get to the West any way they could. At one crossing, a group bribed the Soviet soldiers with Vodka. While it brought immediate results, it eventually turned out to be a big mistake. The group was allowed to cross the border but the soldiers got drunk and then began randomly shooting into the German crowds.

My mother and Sibylle managed to get away, took another road, and came to the autobahn from Berlin to Hannover which was being used by the Western military forces. My sister, young and beautiful, flagged down a British truck while my mother hid behind a bush. The

British soldiers gave them a ride and brought them safely to the West. They were very helpful and preoccupied with my sister and mother's wellbeing, showing the best side of their national character.

The fate of 2 million anti-communist allies of Germany, among them the Russian General Vlassov and his army, was not so kind. They fought for the freedom of their homeland and had to choose between two evils: that of the Nazis, or that of the Communists. They chose what to them seemed like the lesser evil, but the one which was not endorsed by the West. Believing that they were safe in the hands of a Western nation, they laid down their arms and capitulated. Horrifically, Eisenhower then handed them over to the Soviets.

Indescribable scenes, later repeated on other occasions, occurred in Austria. Countless Cossacks committed suicide: men threw themselves in the path of British tanks or ran into machine gun fire; women threw their children into the river and jumped in after them.

In his address on the unveiling of the monument to the Yalta victims in London's Thurloe Square, Member of Parliament Sir Bernard Braine, had the following to say on March 6, 1983: "It was an atrocious crime. I can find no other word to describe what happened. It was committed with violence and deception, without a spark of sympathy for the victims who had willingly handed themselves over to the Western Allies in the belief that they would be granted asylum."

Vlassow was executed as a traitor and I believe that the majority of those who didn't commit suicide before being handed over perished in the manner as my father.

It must be added that Eisenhower also handed over thousands of German soldiers to the Soviets. My close friend, the Roman Catholic priest Engelbert Heller, was among them. When he was released in 1947 because he was unable to work anymore: he weighed 82 pounds. He died in 1991 after suffering decades from a liver illness which he contracted in the Soviet Union. Engelbert was a wonderful Christian and I know where he is now.

Germans numbering 21 million were expulsed from East Germany and Eastern Europe and 2.8 to 3 million of them lost their life in the process. Two million more died of Soviet violence in Central Germany and as prisoners of war in the Soviet Union. Exactly how many of the 11 million German soldiers, taken prisoners of war died is something we shall never know. From the total of 18.2 million soldiers, 5.8 million fell in combat.

The fate of my mother who went to the West in a coal train just as hundreds of thousand other women and children, was described by Bertrand Russell in the following way: "All the time women and children are being herded into railway wagons, each only allowed one suitcase, the contents of which are generally stolen on the way. The journey to Berlin lasts several days, during which no food is distributed. Many are dead when they arrive in Berlin. Children who die on the way are thrown out of the windows."

According to the German magazine "Der Spiegel" historians estimate that 1.4 million women were raped by mobs of Soviet soldiers. My mother and sister were fortunate not to have suffered the same fate.

The first German village reached by the Soviet army was Nemmersdorf. On January 12, 1945, Soviet tanks rolled into this small village in East Prussia and their forces took control of it. Their victory was short lived, however, and it was retaken shortly afterwards by German troops. This is what they found according to an eyewitness: "A ladder wagon stood in the first farmyard on the left side of the street. Four naked women were nailed to it in a crucified position. Behind the 'White Jug Tavern' in the direction of Gumbinnen is an open square with a monument to the Unknown Soldier. Behind that square there is another large tavern. On each of the barn doors, a naked woman had been nailed in a crucified position. In the dwelling houses we then found a total of 37 women and children and one old man who were all dead; most of them had been bestially murdered, except for a few who had been shot in the neck. In one room we found an old lady seated on a sofa. She had been completely blind and was already dead. Half of her head was missing—it had apparently been split off from above with an axe or spade."

This example was not an individual act of passion, rather it was the pattern of the behavior of the victors. Soviet author Ilya Ehrenburg with government assistance encouraged the Soviet soldiers to murder: "Germans are not human beings," he had stated, "we consider the word German to be the basest of all curses. We shall not speak. We shall not become excited. We shall kill. From now on, the word German will be enough to inspire us to shoot…If in the course of a day you do not kill at least one German, kill a second—there is no more pleasant sight for us than German corpses…"

More than 1,000 Soviet military newspapers promoted this philosophy. To make matters worse, Nazi functionaries had forbidden the population to leave their towns and villages until it was nearly too late while they themselves fled, (contrary to what my father had done). It is another disgusting feature of 12 years of Nazi rule.

George F. Kennan observed: "The Russians…swept the native population off the face of the earth in a way which had not been witnessed since the days of the Asian hordes."

I reported already earlier in this book what Putin had said during the 60th anniversary victory celebrations namely that good had defeated evil. I have very seldom heard anything so ridiculous and cynical. I went around Europe to repair relations with our neighbors, apologizing for the crimes of my nation, crimes I had not committed but had helped make possible through my lies and self-centered unchristian life. As I sit here writing my memoirs at the end of November, 2007, I have yet to hear of one Soviet leader that has apologized for the inhumanity and unspeakable crimes of the Soviet Union, its Communist Party, and its armed forces.

The reader can be sure that I know what I am talking about when I say that the Russian leaders of today are not former Communists. They have not changed inside, they are not democrats; they are the same hardcore ruthless Communists with a world-conquering ideology.

They are taking Western leaders for a ride with a new means to hide their motives.

Today, moral subversion not conquering territories is their prime method of attack. They only have put on another label to deceive and defeat us with our help and money; they remain a deadly menace to our freedom. I asked my lawyer in Miami, who only recently came to the United States, what she thought about Putin. Her answer was short and to the point: "Once KGB, always KGB!" Remember, KGB is the Soviet version of our Gestapo and Stasi. Putin called the collapse of the USSR "the greatest geopolitical catastrophe of the last century." Would anybody have allowed "former" Nazis to take leadership positions in Germany and international institutions? Is there a moral difference between a national and an international Socialist, between one ruthless gangster and another one with similar colors?

Bush is being fooled by Putin like Roosevelt was by Stalin, and I can't help but wonder if the president has an advisor like Alger Hiss?

CHAPTER SEVEN

THE YEARS AFTER THE WAR

AS REFUGEES IN THE WEST

THERE WE WERE—a family of four. No longer were we a family of six. Now we found ourselves in a small apartment under the roof of the villa belonging to friends of my parents who owned the local newspaper. Every room in what was now Germany was counted, and each person was allowed a limited footage of room space. If there were less people living in the rooms of a house as per assessed footage, then you had to take in one or more refugees.

Additionally, the bombing had made millions of people homeless and they all had to be accommodated one way or the other. In comparison to others, our family was very fortunate to have the privacy that came with living in the house of friends. My mother had managed to obtain the furniture and other essentials from her sister who had died in the last days of the war. We again had some possessions and were off to a flying start—or so we thought!

Any plan I had for my life was completely derailed by the war and I didn't have the slightest idea of what I should do now. A career as a military officer was not possible anymore because Germany no longer had an army. Nothing else really attracted me and the concept of working for money was abhorrent.

The joy of life had left my mother and even though she couldn't accept it, she had to admit to herself that my father was not coming back again. In the absence of any purpose, she became depressed, which in turn depressed us all. It didn't help to be confronted with the physical destruction of our country, the crimes of the Hitler gang, the Holocaust, and the murder of millions of others.

I loafed around without any real reason to live my life. After coming back from the war I had to be officially dismissed by the occupation power, which in our case was Great Britain. They classified you according to your involvement with the Nazis. It started with "criminal" and ended with "having a clear record." Basically all Germans were considered to be Nazis, which infuriated me. Adding insult to injury, the British felt they had to educate us, which made me even more furious. There were various degrees of their involvement cited but the bottom line was, whether or not they granted your dismissal from the army. Without it you couldn't do much and it was something like not having a social security number here in America in the years before illegal immigrants flooded the country. I got my dismissal without problem.

My mother told us later that only the existence of her children saved her from suicide, the despair was so great. We may have been her purpose, but I still had none. Burchard had gone back to high school to take his final examination—Abitur. Sibylle was working on a farm nearby, but I still remained up in the air. My mother realized that her task was to provide us with a center and give us the backing of a family, a task she accomplished in a wonderful way!

I am ashamed to confess that I had very little initiative leading my mother to look for work for me. One job I got, I remember, was to be the driver for the head of the Rudolph Oetker Company, a well-known big business. I had obtained my three drivers licenses, motor cycle, car, and truck in the Army, but besides the hours during training, I had never driven a car. Among the many mistakes this poor man had to suffer because of me, the worst took place one morning on the way to the office when I drove him into a ditch and couldn't get the car out. If I remember correctly, that was the end of my career as a driver.

CLASH WITH THE BRITISH ARMY

Following my stint as a driver, I found work in the automobile repair shop of the British Army which employed three or four German civilians in its office. I can't remember what exactly I had to do, but recall that the high point of each day was when the sergeant in charge of the office came around and offered everybody an English cigarette.

While German cigarettes did not arouse great excitement, American and English cigarettes had a hefty black market value of five marks at that time. Because of their value, these cigarettes became a standard of currency determining the value of merchandise like bread, meat, and coffee. I cannot remember anybody being interested in the French cigarettes.

One day, and I do not remember how this conversation started, a British soldier, who was a Scotsman and a head smaller than I, told me that he would hang me in the next war. I looked down on him and answered with a sneer, that it would need about half a dozen men of his size to achieve it. He got angry and challenged me to follow him outside so that we could settle the matter right away.

As I followed him to where we were to have our fight, he told me about the many brawls he had been in and how sometimes he had smashed a bottle of beer on the head of his opponents. He also showed me some scars on his head that confirmed the many fights he had been in. My stomach grew queasy as he asked me if I preferred boxing or wrestling. I thought that boxing might be somewhat bloody and painful, and therefore I chose wrestling. We agreed that we were going to go the best out of three rounds.

As soon as we reached a suitable place to have our fight, we immediately dove into the first round. To my surprise, it didn't take me very long to pin him. Just when we wanted to get into the second round, British military police appeared on the scene. I was arrested and thrown into prison. This, however, was a German prison—not a regular one but more something like what a police station might have. It was an "investigation" prison where you are put in before sentencing.

My family found out quickly what had happened and made contact with me from the street. I was looking out through the window of my cell. What do I need? I asked for a Bible and my washroom bag. To be honest, both were supposed to hide cigarettes, which my family had concealed on my request. The cigarettes made it through and I shared them with the other inmates via the prison guard.

Two days later two officers of the British Secret Service came to the prison and interrogated me. But more than anything they wanted to explain to me that they had no choice but to arrest me because somebody from an occupied country cannot fight a soldier of the occupation force. I satisfied them by promising that I would never fight another British soldier, and I was set free. That was the end of my career as an employee of the British Army.

THE CUCUMBER STEALING

After that I was hired by the manager of a nursery near Aurich in Ostfriesland who had known my parents and wanted to help us. The company grew tomatoes in the field, and cucumbers in glasshouses. At the end of the first workday in one glasshouse I noticed how some workers would hide cucumbers under their jackets and leave. It didn't take me long to find out that they sold the stolen cucumbers outside the plant to displaced persons, who waited there for them. These were people who had been forced to come to Germany to work, replacing the German men who served in the armed forces. Most of those who came from Eastern Europe didn't want to return because the communists were in charge in their homelands, and stayed in camps until their emigration to other countries was cleared. They were on rations like the British and

American armies and had plenty of cigarettes, coffee and whatever else one desired.

At the one gate through which everybody had to leave the plant stood guards who would arbitrarily search some of the workers for stolen goods. If they found cucumbers or tomatoes on someone, that person would be fired immediately. I thought that the risk was too high for just two or three stolen cucumbers valued at ten to fifteen cigarettes.

I began to study the area and found out that each glasshouse had a vent to the outside part of the plant used for air circulation. I stayed in a bed and breakfast place about 200 yards away from those glasshouses and their vents. The ground was covered by bushes and there was a small path starting at the end of one glasshouse that led straight to my place. It was perfect, I could enter and leave the plant without inspection and nobody would see me. I would pilfer the cucumbers and reach my room in the bed and breakfast completely undetected.

Today I still shudder to think of what a calculating thief I became, but I wasted no time and sprung into action the next day. During breakfast and lunch breaks, and at the end of the day I would throw about 20 cucumbers through the vents into the bushes, pick them up later outside, and bring them into my room. I was in big business moving about 300 cucumbers per week and receiving the buyers in my room. On weekends I would travel to the North Sea island of Norderney and have a great time.

I had no sense of guilt and my conscience was numb to the wrong I was doing. Of course I did not regard myself as a thief, which I was, and instead convinced myself that society had treated my family and me badly justifying my unscrupulous conduct. My racket didn't last, however, because I left the plant only few weeks after arrival.

THE POWER OF HATRED

Something strange was happening on the ground floor of our house in Halle early in 1946. The inhabitants of the first floor then told us that the whole villa had been confiscated by the British army to serve as an officer's mess. There was a captain down there, they told us, confiscating furniture and other belongings of the inhabitants. The same thing had happened to my grandmother in another city nearly a year earlier. We managed to push some items into the attic, which was not part of our home, and covered its entry with a sofa.

A riding whip under his arm, this captain marched into our living area with his secretary in tow. Taking no notice of us, he surveyed our belongings like we didn't exist and indicated to his secretary that practically all of our newly acquired furniture was to be confiscated. Then he left as arrogantly as he came, as if we had no more value than the dust on the furniture.

My mother was white with rage as the secretary informed us that we had 24 hours to leave and were not allowed to take the confiscated items with us. We defined the matter in this way: "To love your neighbor is a Christian duty. To hate the British is a national concern." Our hearts were heavy, our minds were muddled, and there was more of this injustice to come.

Twenty-four hours later, close friends of ours sent us a horse wagon where we loaded what was left of our newly acquired belongings. Once we filled the wagon, we rode to their castle nearby, where they had cleared two big rooms for our family. The castle was already filled with the family and refugees, among them a number of very nice girls. In spite of my aimless drifting I had a great time when we lived with these warm-hearted and generous people.

They belonged to the Catholic high nobility while we were Lutheran lower nobility. The uncle of the countess Maria von Korff Schmising was the Cardinal Count von Galen, who was well known in Germany through his public opposition to the Nazi persecution of Jews. There was a chapel in the castle and I got accustomed to participating in Sunday mass while we lived there. And even though I lived a miserable immoral life, I consider this as a season of preparation for life where I learned to look first and foremost into the Christian substance in people and not at their dogmas.

Our Landlords

Though it had taken her quite some time to establish her right, my mother eventually got a small government pension because of my father's public service. She had not taken any documents with her when she was driven from our home in Freiwaldau and so had to weave her way through a maze of post-war bureaucracy to verify her entitlement to the money. That pension, however, didn't cover the need of the family, and we continued to struggle financially as neither my brother nor I had a career or a job.

In her youth my mother had learned to be midwife but never worked in that capacity. Amazingly, she discovered an opening for a midwife nearby and applied for the position. The job included an apartment in Brockhagen, about three miles away from the castle, and she was hired. Our move to this village, where we would spend the next couple of years, was immediate. Her work not only provided an income but since most of the women she delivered babies for were the wives of farmers, we often received food as well.

Officially, food was rationed and purchased by using government coupons sent each month. The irony of the government provisions was that there was too little food to live on yet too much food to die with. The result was that people who lived in the city would swarm across the countryside trying to sell their belongings for food.

Though we now had improved our position, my mother continued to struggle with her pride. For example, when she attended the first baptism of a child that she had brought into the world, the child's father, who was a farmer, gave her a tip as was the custom. She had never been tipped before in her life and almost gave the money back to him. However, because of her children's need for any kind of education possible, she swallowed her pride and accepted the gift. From that point on she would return from all baptisms with food and money.

The couple who owned the house with our apartment, the Kochbecks, had a cow housed in a stable that was actually part of the house. Additionally, there was just one toilet for the whole house, which everybody had to use. It was a primitive facility that worked without water, a Plumps Klo, as we called it, and it was located just opposite of the cow.

Whenever we had to relieve ourselves, we had to come down the staircase and go through the stable area to get into the Klo. At night of course, we had to light the staircase and the stable which drew from the Kochbecks electricity instead of ours. In an effort to save money, when anyone of us came down to use the toilet at night, the light was usually turned off by the time we came out. Consequently we wound up with our share of bumps and bruises, often hitting our head or shinbone on something before being able to turn the light on again.

Herr Kochbeck was a worker in a nearby factory and left very early, around 5:00am. He rode a motorcycle which made tremendous racket that woke us all up. We went to bed fairly late and my mother normally lay awake for hours due to the turmoil within before falling asleep early in the morning. Herr Kochbeck's motorcycle almost always woke her just after she had dozed off and made impossible for her to fall back asleep.

Coffee was a luxury very few could afford in those post-war years, certainly not the common man. The popular method of making coffee at that time was: boil water, take one bean of coffee, and pour the boiling water over it into a cup. Then enjoy your cup of "coffee."

Our bathroom, on the other hand, was over the Kochbecks' bedroom, and the water pipes ran through the wall behind the heads of their beds. Just as the noise of Herr Kochbeck's motorcycle woke us up, the water rushing down behind him woke him up as well. They begged us to wash at an earlier time but we ignored them, resenting the fact that we had to live in such a place. They, in turn, resented our arrogance leading Herr Kochbeck to actually put little flags in the garden where our Dachshund Purzel had done his business. It was meant to demonstrate how impossible it was to live with us.

Both our families were Lutherans and on Sundays we went to the only church in the village—but never together. We did not call our feelings hatred but rather justified annoyance. But truthfully, it was hatred which infested our hearts and the house where we so-called Christians lived a million miles from each other though we were physically near enough to reach out and hold hands. When we prayed the Lord's Prayer in the church or at home and said "and forgive us our trespasses as we forgive those who trespass against us," we never made the connection between what we said with our lips and the reality of our lives.

THE NAZI ISSUE HAUNTS US

We thought that we were getting rich! My mother needed transportation to get back and forth to work so she bought a light motor cycle. When all of us went anywhere together on the weekend, mother would leave with the motorcycle and we would walk. After having covered some distance, my mother would leave the motorcycle on the side of the road and continue walking. When we reached the motorcycle the first one of us would drive it until reaching our mother. Then he or she would again leave our means of transportation on the side of the road and walk along with mother until the next of us caught up and did the same. Soon we were able to buy an additional bicycle, and were very pleased with the progress we were making as we rebuilt our lives from scratch.

One day my uncle Adolf came to visit us whom I have mentioned earlier. As soon as my uncle had entered our home, my mother lashed out at him. "You Nazi," she cried, "Look what you have done to our country and to our family." He slowly put his monocle on to his right eye, looked straight at my mother, and answered, "It is because of reactionaries like you that we lost the war." He had learned nothing through the terrors of war, and didn't learn until he died.

Like everyone else, we had followed developments covered by the news media, especially the Nurnberg War Criminal Trials. Most of those accused of crimes got what they deserved but not all. A lot of the background information I elaborate on in this book, I learned later on in life. What we disliked thoroughly right from the beginning, however, was to see the Soviets among the judges and prosecutors. We knew who and what they were, Stalin was, and the horrific crimes and mass murders the communists had committed long before Hitler came to power. And every German knew the manifold ruthless crimes the Red Army had performed against the East German population, especially against women and children. So what you had was comparable to Mafia Godfathers sitting in judgment of common criminals and it echoed through our hearts like nails scratching across a chalkboard.

The Soviet prosecutor accused Germany of having murdered 15,000 Polish officers in Katyn after the war during their occupation of Poland. A mass grave with 4,000 of them was found near Katyn. As well as the German military, the prosecutor knew very well that this mass murder was committed by the Soviets themselves and not by the Germans. And yet, not surprisingly, it didn't bother him to make innocent people suffer. I do not remember the details, but I think American intelligence had been aware of the facts. The charges were dropped. Still Germany was not cleared and the Soviets continued to sit in judgment of their fellow gangsters. Again, I have never heard of any Soviet leader apologizing to the Poles or to us for that matter.

Ultimately, America and Britain did not stand up for their own principles. Rejecting German resistance and teaming up with Stalin, a bloodthirsty butcher makes any thinking people wonder what Western society really stands for. Impressive double talk and the application of variable standards to people and nations that support political interests rather than integrity, does not create justice, enact sound policy, or make friends.

At the same time the American people flooded Germany with Care parcels right after the war was over. The ordinary warm-hearted

American could not just watch the misery of people and a whole nation without doing something about it. I will never forget the air bridge to Berlin from June to December 1948 when the planes of the American Air force flew supplies into Berlin. The Soviets had unsuccessfully tried to force the Western powers out of Berlin by cutting the road connections to West-Germany. The Marshall Plan put Germany back on her economic feet. Chancellor Konrad Adenauer traveled to Washington to thank the American government and people for their help. "It is the first time in history," he stated, "that a victorious nation helps the former enemy in such generous way to recover from the wounds of war."

In 1995 my friend Alfred Champion, business man and retired Colonel took me to a breakfast of The Retired Officers Association (TROA) in Colorado Springs where we lived. After we had finished eating, the guest speaker spoke on the Holocaust and a spirited dialog followed which was chaired by Major General (ret.) John H. Mitchell. Numerous soldiers in attendance pressed for a clear cut answer to why the United States had entered the war. At the end of the discussion the only conclusion that could be drawn was that there simply was no rational explanation for how an atrocity as sweeping as the Holocaust could be committed by a cultured nation like Germany.

As the discussion developed I debated within whether I should try to say something since I could explain what had happened. Just before General Mitchell closed the event I raised my hand and before I knew it I stood on the platform before the microphone. I thanked the retired officers for the freedom which American soldiers had made available to me through their grit and with their blood, destroying the Nazi regime. Then I explained to them the same way I have in this book how the Nazi atrocities and the Holocaust were made possible. I will never forget the thunderous applause I received or the honor I still feel to have been made an honorary member of the association.

Dr. James Dobson, founder and then president of Focus on the Family, heard about the event and invited me to be with him on his national radio program remembering the anniversary of the end of World

War II. I felt honored and humbled by the invitation to appear on a broadcast that reached millions of people.

During the Nineties I became a board member of "The Day the Wall Came Down," a project created to strengthen the American-German friendship. The United States Air Force joined with the German Luftwaffe to fly a sculpture of five horses by Veryl Goodnight as a symbol of freedom to Berlin. Former President Bush unveiled the monument in the presence of the Lord Mayor of Berlin, a member of the German government, and our board, headed by Major General (ret.) John Mitchell, commander of Berlin from 1984–88.

A great many German soldiers who returned home from the war, many of them several years after its end, were thoroughly confused. We didn't understand what had happened to us. The Nazi crimes were horrible, and they could not be denied due to public knowledge but no one knew if and how one was responsible. For six years the German soldier had put up a tremendous fight against a world of enemies; any army could be proud of such personal loyalty and a military feat. Like me, most did not fight for Nazi ideology or the quest for world domination, but for our country. Nearly six million of our soldiers—including my brother—had died in combat. Survivors returned home after humiliating months and years as prisoners of war (not those who were fortunate enough to be POWs in the USA) and found themselves being accused of being part of a Nazi criminal conspiracy.

Most of them were never afforded the luxury or closure of a realistic explanation. I don't know to how many children of veterans I have talked who told me that their father never spoke to them about the war and what he thought about it. These fathers knew as I did that we fought to defend our country but struggled in vain to connect those motives with the Nazi criminal evidence. It is because of this impossible contradiction that they pushed the events and experiences of those years unresolved into their sub-consciences and successfully got to work on the reconstruction of the country—again to the wonder of the watching world.

I have always believed that Germany as a nation has never reconciled the puzzle of our Nazi past. Therefore, we are constantly being blackmailed, paying and paying and paying with higher quotas in international institutions than anybody else, always vulnerable, always seeking but never finding an answer. Germans of all generations carry a mountainous burden of guilt, and the country is once again sliding into the grinding jaws of totalitarian rule.

For me the question, "How was it possible?" thrust itself into the forefront of my mind and hounded me. How was it possible, that a cultured nation with millions of Christians going to church every Sunday and espousing the highest moral standards known to humanity could be a epicenter of such inhumanity, of such crimes? After having shared with the reader a number of my un-Christian acts you might wonder how on earth I could take a Christian point of view in my attempt to find an answer. Don't worry, there are more un-Christian acts to come and when you have read the whole story you should be able to get the picture.

HAMBURG UNIVERSITY

Slowly and painfully my life returned to the new normal. Our beloved friends, who had taken us into their home when we were thrown onto the street by the British army, again came forward to help us. Uncle Clemens, Count von Korff Schmising, offered to pay for my education, if I was interested in learning languages. Of course I was, and so I set out to get myself an English and Spanish interpreter certificate from the Berlitz School in Bielefeld, about 12 miles away from where we lived. For eight months I attended daily classes and ultimately the basics of these two languages became the foundation of much of my future life. They made me an attractive business prospect much later, helped me understand other cultures, and make friends with people. More importantly however, they helped me to make myself understood by the most beautiful person I ever met, a gorgeous Peruvian girl who I am happy to say married me.

The only way I could get to my classes in Bielefeld without wasting time was by bicycle. At that time there were no trucks which drove very fast and though they went at a reasonable speed, they had to stop at red lights like everybody else.

What I did to conserve energy was to wait at a traffic light until a truck had to stop in front of me and hang on to the rear right-hand-side of the truck with my left hand so it could pull me to my destination. It was normally successful because the drivers, while aware of this were conscious of the needs of others and helped them out if they could.

Meanwhile my mother had talked to all her friends seeking advice about how to get her son started in a career. Her best girlfriend from school had married Hugo Homann, the owner of a margarine factory. Homann had connections to the Unilever Concern, and before I knew it I was an apprentice in their national headquarters in Hamburg. In Germany, the Company was known as the Margarine Union.

As time passed, my mother strengthened her financial position and between her pension and income, she was able to encourage me to seek an academic degree. I wasn't quite sure what degree to pursue, much less what to do once I earned it, but in the end I came to the conclusion that economics couldn't do me any harm.

I have to admit that I really wasn't very interested because I didn't know what to do with my life and post-war Germany had nothing especially exciting to offer me. I had a room in Blankenese, a suburb about half an hour ride on the S-Bahn (speedy train) to the university and the Unilever offices. I joined a student corporation where fencing was obligatory. This was a kind of bloody affair since the target was the face of the opponent from another corporation. A helmet protected one's eyes and top of the head but left the nose and cheeks exposed. The point of this century-old student tradition is to prove that you can overcome your fear. I became chairman of our organization but was less and less convinced that I was doing the right thing. After all, I said to myself, I am a veteran and was in combat, why should I prove to anybody that I am not afraid? So eventually I left it but remained close to my friends.

At the university I am sorry to say that I continued with the same immoral values that led me to steal cucumbers earlier. Students were required to register for the courses they wanted to take and in order to sit for final exams you had to have both registered and passed all required courses with an acceptable grade. Six written essays on the subjects given to you by the professors were mandatory and after four semesters I had written five essays with acceptable results.

Shamefully, I did not pass any of these exams as a result of hard work and study. Instead, I had taken the easy way out and cheated on all of them, each time in a new and creative way. Rather late in my tenure as a student, I realized that I was mostly harming myself and got serious about learning. The intellectual damage was so extensive at this point though that some of my friends thought I would never graduate.

I bought a monthly second-class ticket for the S-Bahn to go from Blankenese to the university. The train in the morning as in the evening was so full that there was scarcely space to stand. Because they were expensive, first class compartments were empty. Of course I thought I would be better off there though I didn't have the money, so true to form, I devised a scheme to accommodate my desire. I bought myself a single first class ticket in addition to the monthly ticket and using a hammer I cautiously made the date on it illegible.

Thus I went with my monthly ticket through control and then sat comfortably in the first class compartment. Occasionally I had to deal with the scrutiny of the controller who was on to me and marked the ticket. I didn't let that stop me however and simply bought myself a new one and continued with the same scam.

No wonder that nothing seemed to give me satisfaction or direction in life. I was staggering from day to day and from month to month and had no idea what my purpose in life was, or where to go to find it. We didn't talk very much about the war or our country even though most of us in the student corporation were veterans. We were burnt out. Still, thinking of my country today and the Nazi regime then perturbed me trying to find answers to the question, "How was it possible." It was like trying to catch the wind. I knew everything was wrong with Germany, I suspected that something must be very wrong with me, but I couldn't put my finger on anything concrete. Try as I might I could not connect my disjointed life, past, present, and future, with God or the fate of Germany, not to speak of the entire world.

It was at this point, however, that I began to realize every human being needs a reason to live, a purpose bigger than their self. Religion did not offer any challenge and what I heard in my church most likely was all true, but in its biblical precision, it was boring and seemed detached from real life. I was reduced to a walking corpse with only self at the center of my life, and unable to distinguish between right and wrong.

THE WINDS OF CHANGE

Finally, in the summer of 1949, my life began to change. I met a British journalist in Switzerland who was very different from all the Englishmen I had met previously. I was on my way to Salzburg in Austria to visit a girl that I was very interested in. But first I went to Zuerich to visit the Steinfels family. Our families had been friends for two generations and I was the third. My grandmother had been in the same class with the mother of Fritz Steinfels in a boarding school for girls in Lausanne, Switzerland, before World War I. The Steinfels were the ones my parents visited in 1936 and they were also the first ones to send us food parcels after the war as soon as they knew where we were.

Through Fritz I met Peter Howard, a London Fleet Street journalist who had been the right hand man of Lord Beaverbrook. Beaverbrook was a well-known newspaper magnate and politician. He had been a member of Churchill's war cabinet in various positions. Howard was a warm hearted, outgoing person who possessed an uncommon humility and treated others, including me (a former enemy), with respect. His life was guided in part by his vision of how the world should be and what needed to change. I was fascinated. He seemed to believe that his own country, Great Britain, sat on a heap of sins and needed more change than any other country. Never had I heard a man speak like this before.

The post-war world was inundated with publicity that hyped Germany as the only nation in the world which was a criminal nation. If any country and any people needed to change for the better, it was Germany and the Germans (who were all categorized as Nazi). And of course, because I knew the virtue and good of the people as well as our darker side, I was determined never to admit anything of this nature to anybody, especially our British re-educators. Yet here I saw and heard an Englishman serious about the need of his country to embrace profound moral change. He pointed out exactly where, and shared his own personal sins. He made jokes about the "stiff upper lip" and many British cultural nuances. At the same time he showed me his appreciation for Germany and for myself. He struck a nerve and I was shaken, wanting to cheer him on as something began to awaken deep inside of me. You don't hate somebody you feel cheerful about.

Through him I met another astounding person, a French woman, Irene Laure. She was the secretary general of the Socialist women of France and had been in the French resistance during the war. The Gestapo understandably led her to hate the Germans who had tortured her son. That I could appreciate, but I didn't know what to say. Before, I had always maintained that I had committed no crimes, that I had killed no Jews, that I had fought for my country like everybody else in whatever nation and that therefore anybody who looked for those who were responsible for the German crimes should focus on someone else, but not at me because I was innocent.

Irene Laure told me how she had lost her hatred and started on her level to work with German leaders. I was told that she played a major role in the reconciliation between France and Germany, which was progressing vigorously in those years.

I was shaken even more. Peter Howard told me that hatred was not only wrong but stupid. How can anybody hate another nation, another class, another race or any other group without even knowing most of those he hates? "Hatred is destructive," he reasoned. "It ties the persons who hate to the object of their hatred causing them to become slaves of their hatred."

He went on, "Furthermore, hatred means insulting God, who commands us to love our neighbor." Even though I had heard this truth before, this time it was different. I wasn't being preached at—somebody was sharing an experience with me, and that made it more than a religious truth—it made it true and THAT eclipsed religion.

LISTEN TO GOD

Then I met Arthur Richter. I never knew what his profession was but did discover that he came from Hannover, the same area where my family came from. He was an evangelist, and had an almost chilling insight into human nature. What I mean by that is he could look through my endless argumentations and see the reality of a desperate and lost human being. He asked me whether I believed in God. "Of course," I answered, "I am a Christian, and I go to church on Sundays." I can hear the laughter of true believers who have read those stories I described earlier. "How on earth can a person, committing such horrendous acts of paganism, seriously believe that he is a Christian?" It didn't take very long, and I was incredulously asking myself his very intimidating question.

"Have you ever listened to God?" was the next question. "Listen to God," I said, "what do you mean? God of course doesn't have the time to speak to billions of people on the earth. But I pray." That was a lie, I didn't pray normally with the exception of the official prayers in church. I was sure of myself and felt that I was on safe ground—until the earthquake began to rock my world. "Did you try it at least?" he asked. I was defensive and getting irritated as I felt myself cornered. "Don't you think that since we have two ears and only one mouth that we should listen to God twice as much than we pray to Him?" He shot back at me. I couldn't deny the logic of that thought and was at a loss to respond.

I can't remember how long it took until I finally gave-in. I sat down in my room with a pad of paper and a pen and did what Arthur had told me I should do: ask God to help me write down the thoughts and sins that came to my mind—without editing. I looked at myself through the eyes of God. That means that I looked at my life and how I had lived and treated other people, applying the standard of God's moral absolutes, absolute honesty, absolute purity, absolute unselfishness, and absolute love. I had learned this much, God was truth and truth had to be absolute otherwise it would adapt to different people. I learned that irrespective of nation, class, color, or religion God's standards are the same for every last person on earth.

The truth about me and who I am came now to the light of the day. The first thought that came to mind was "I don't believe it." I wrote it down. The next thought was "whore." I knew what it meant. Once as a soldier, I had gone to a whore, not because I really wanted to, but because I wanted to prove something to my fellow soldiers. It was as if somebody yanked a curtain away from my eyes letting in the glow of reality suddenly shine into the darkest corners of my corrupted soul revealing horror and reality of what sin is. For until then God and sin were only intellectual concepts for me but not reality. Now I was face to face with reality, the reality of me as I faced truth.

The walls within me came tumbling down as my defenses fell, and I was flooded with the sins I had committed. I do not remember how long it took to write them down or how many pages I filled, but the man I saw was terrible. My lies, my cheating, my fraud, my stealing, my indifference to the rights and needs of others, my arrogance—how on earth could I feel superior to anybody? How could I think that I was a Christian? I thought of those two Hungarian women and wept with shame. When my evangelical friend joined me later I read to him the whole register of my insults to God. That was even worse than writing them down. I fell to my knees, asked God to forgive me, and Jesus to wash me. I surrendered my life to God then and there. I don't know how I could have continued to live with myself without the cleansing power of the blood of Jesus Christ.

I also saw the reality of what people of other nations felt about us Germans and Germany, and had to admit to myself, that if all Germans were like me, that it was no wonder the Nazis could manipulate the morally compromised non-Nazis and get their way. For the first time I could see the connection between the Nazis, their crimes, and me.

I had not lived up to my moral obligations as a Christian. I had lied, cheated and seen nothing wrong with the way the Nazis had treated the Jews. I had lied for comparatively trivial personal gains, they had lied for political power, and I was no better. My lies had joined me to them who had lied to us about everything. I had been a Christian fraud, a bystander who saw no evil. Now I had to face evil in myself and the moral responsibility for what had happened as a result of millions living similar to the way I did.

I had not felt superior to others because of race but because of being an aristocrat. Nonetheless, the arrogance was the same even though I didn't murder others because of it. Arrogant pride was at the heart of my being. Disgusted with myself, I tore my family ring with our coat of arms from my finger and threw it out of the window. However, I realized quickly that there is a difference between arrogance and pride in your nation, your traditions, and your family of which you are a part. Thankfully, I found my ring in the garden the next day and I am still wearing it as I pen these memoirs. But my arrogance has been crucified in Christ and I am a new man still.

Knowing now what kind of person I was and comparing it to the person I had pretended to be I began to learn to look through appearances of others and find the real person behind the front as well as the reality of his or her motives. What matters most is not what a person says for as the saying goes, "talk is cheap," but what the motives are which drive a person.

WHO RUNS THE NATION?

I had entered into an astounding new life with a new and different outlook and the knowledge and experience how anybody else could have the same experience. Then I began connecting what I had learned to my shattered nation and its wounded spirit. I looked for a resurrection of my frustrated and unhappy land, so that it could find a way to come to terms with the past and find the road to the future. From the outset, my personal life was interwoven with the life of Germany. It became clear to me that every person of course must live his or her individual life. However, the way he or she lives has either a positive or negative impact on their nation. Thus, the individual and the nation have to be considered as one and cannot be separated. A nation is no more than its people; so as I am, so is my nation.

And then of course there is God. How was it possible for a German government to commit these horrendous crimes, lead our nation into total destruction, cause the suffering and death of millions of people, and burden the nation with crushing guilt for generations to come? How could all this be possible in a nation that included millions of church-going Christians? How could they not have had an impact on the nation's direction? Why did those who say they love God, not guide the nation but instead allow unrestrained godless monsters to dictate events?

I had found the answer to that question, "How was it possible?"— most Christians were like me. I went to church, but I was not a Christian. I didn't love God, and neither did they, no matter what they said, because the only way to express your love for God and for Jesus is by obeying our creator's Commandments, and by making them the basis for your national life. And that includes the fight to bring the social and political structures of society in accordance with those moral absolutes. This we did not do. We had no bigger purpose than self, a purpose that included trying to get into heaven.

Godlessness was and still is the central problem of Germany. And the answer to that godlessness is not more religion or more spirituality in society—it is obedience to God. Our concept of the Christian religion and God are not identical. I am the living proof to this thesis and so is Germany.

The Nazi government had excluded God from their consideration. To exclude God and his Commandments from human government is a heresy promoted by the godless in order to gain their own power. Gutless church-goers allow it to happen. Would the creator of Heaven and Earth, the creator of every last person in this world, exempt from His standards those who govern the nations? Any rational person should be able to conclude that this would be complete nonsense. But it was and is reality. It is the duty of every Christian to make sure that their government abides by the Commandments of their Creator. If German church-goers had abided by that rule, the Nazis could not have committed their crimes. Unfortunately, I have to say, I cannot see the majority of American Christians living by that rule either. I shall come back to this issue later in this book.

The first thing I did after I had given my life to God was to apologize to Peter Howard in representation of the British people for the hatred I had nourished. I told him that my commitment to God meant that I would never again be a bystander but fight for the truth of God. I couldn't have found a warmer reception of my stammered words and even though I rarely saw him, he was a friend. To this day, some of my best friends were and are British.

All of this happened when Fritz Steinfels took me to the Mountain House in Caux located in Switzerland. We attended the conference center of Moral Rearmament, during an international conference with attendance of about a thousand people.

Baptism of Baby Sibylle celebration, May 23, 1927. From top left: Hilmar's parents, Alfred and Margarete; grandfather, Friedrich von Campe; maternal grandfather, Hans Wesener; family doctor, Diering.

Next Line: friends, Hugo and Emmy Homann; brother-in-law, Adolf Wolf; cousins, Kurt and Thea Hesse.

Next Line: Mother's sister, Martha Wesener with Baby Asche; maternal grandmother Anna with Baby Hilmar; great grandmother, von Wedelstaedt; grandmother von Campe with just-baptized Baby Sibylle; sister of mother, Lily Wolf.

Hilmar wearing the Hitlar Youth uniform, 1936.

Mother with her four children, 1938. From left: Burchard, Hilmar, Asche and Sibylle.

Brother Asche, 1942.

Hilmar in a line of soldiers, 1943. Third from the right.

Mother with 69 years, 1966.

Hilmar as a young soldier wearing the tank uniform, 1944.

The von Campe family, 1937. From left: Mother, Asche, Burchard, Hilmar, Sibylle, Father.

Our family at Christmas 2007. From left to right. Back row: Stefan, Hilmar, Dina. Front row: Marcelo, Sabrina, Sophie.

A New Family

When I came home, I didn't say much to my mother and sister about my experience in Switzerland at first. Burchard lived in Hannover at that time. When I got up after lunch with them and went to wash the dishes, there were no machines at that time, they were speechless and knew immediately that something must have happened to me. I had never done anything like this before and had been an extreme example of an arrogant male chauvinist without ever taking responsibility for anything in the household.

Since there were very few cigarettes to buy the first three years after the war, everybody who could do so planted and produced his own tobacco and consequently cigarettes. My mother and sister on the other hand planted potatoes and vegetables in our small lot of land. When I watered my tobacco, I had never bothered to water their garden though it was right next to mine. It was not a separation of church and state but of male and female responsibilities according to my distorted thinking. Now I was so ashamed, that I apologized to them for my heartless indifference and exploiting them and backed up my words with action.

When I finally told them about my change of heart and purpose explaining my misdeeds to them, both got the point quickly and realized that I was trying to change them as well. It was exactly what I had in mind to be honest, but my mother was furious lamenting to our friends that her son had no respect for his mother by trying to change her. Since she used the same kind of arguments I had used in trying to fend off the challenge, and I knew how miserable she was in her heart, I kept at it.

My efforts were rewarded as the day dawned when she recognized how wrong her hatred was. Suddenly she realized that she was a hypocrite pretending to be a Christian, and that she needed to change, change not only just letting go of her hatred, but also apologizing to those she had hated. That, however, was too much for her. She was ready to apologize to our landlord and to the British; however, forgiving the Nazis was a completely different story. Her hatred of the Nazis was deep seated for she felt that they had destroyed her family, her life, and our country causing her blood to boil when she thought about forgiving them.

Finally, realizing the power of her hatred and need for God to vanquish it she fell to her knees and cried to the Lord, "I know that my hatred is wrong, but I am unable to get rid of it. I shall not get up until you have liberated me from it. Please help me." She stayed on her knees and prayed for two hours, after which she got up a free and happy woman, who had accepted the loss of her husband and destruction of our family and country without bitterness. She also gave her life to God with a commitment to fight for His truth in people and in the nation. She wanted to make a difference in the world and that is what she did for the next 15 years, a fulfilled woman with a mission and a destiny. What more can a son wish for his mother?

She died in 1966. Her burial service was officiated by Pastor Dr. Klaus Bockmuehl who said, "When we today say goodbye to Margarete von Campe our thoughts must be directed to the purpose of her life, what was she living for? What does any human live for? That is the most important question one can ask regarding the life of any person, and the answer to that question will show us the character of this person. Margarete von Campe lived for bringing God back to Germany. God in Germany!"

It is sad that Germany did not follow the same path as my mother. The fact that the majority of a socialist/green government including former Chancellor Schroeder and former Foreign Minister Fischer, left any reference to God out of their oath of office and were never-the-less elected to a second term demonstrates the fact that neither they nor those who elected them understand the nature of the Nazi disaster. According to a poll in February of 2005, 48 percent of Germans want to abolish religion in school in favor of mathematics and German language. The same ignorance resulted in the victory of the French initiative to leave God out of the new European Constitution, which was accepted by the majority of the European governments. As it now develops, that may not be the last word on the matter. People get afraid of losing their national identity and of an invasion of immigrants, aliens of our culture. A leading Christian Democrat, Wolfgang Schaeuble, minister of interior in the Merkel government, was asked by a journalist for a commentary on the ouster of God in the new European Constitution. He answered, that he would have liked to have a reference to God but that they had not been successful in trying.

I am not impressed by such a lukewarm approach to the issue and since there are too many of his colleagues of similar mediocrity, the path of Europe is on a steep and slippery slide leading to the totalitarian disaster that produced Hitler. Any American leader needs to know what he or she is dealing with in Europe. More religion is not the answer—Schaeuble and his party friends have religion, even Christian religion to be exact, but what they lack is God who is truth and power. But His power is of different nature than the political manipulations of present day governments. His power is truth and it must be applied by governments.

He who wants to fight for truth and doesn't quite know how and what truth is must first define evil. Then he or she must fight the evil they recognize because otherwise truth cannot reign. In our family, we recognized and defined the evil most disturbing to us, that which filled our hearts and we had to deal with it. That brings me to say that only those who first look at themselves with God's eyes can find truth, everything else is intellectual chatter. They also will experience the reality of the statement of Jesus Christ when He said "I am the way, the truth, and the life."

A patriot is he who faces God's absolute truth about his country after having faced himself and then joins those who fight to correct what is morally wrong. Everybody wants the other fellow, the other nation, the other group, those with a different religion or race to be different or killed first. This erroneous philosophy led to all materialistic ideologies, ideologies that only make things worse. "If you point your finger at your neighbor, there are four pointing back at you," the saying goes. Lasting change, as I found out, must begin with oneself and one's own nation. Millions of marriages break up because each part blames the other and neither wants to change.

RESTITUTION

All of us three in the family took our time to make restitution where we had hurt people. I needed several months. I went to all my professors, confessed my cheating and apologized. I had to repeat only one exam. One professor, who was close to retirement, was amazed at my honesty. He said that this was the first time a student had confessed cheating in his class. Little did he know about what went on in the classroom. I wrote to the railway management, to the president of the cucumber company, and many others; even the press got hold of the story. I could not make restitution to the two Hungarian women, I could only ask God to forgive me.

All of us three went to our landlords, the Kochbecks, and apologized for our arrogance and indifference. It was amazing, they responded warmly and we became friends. After we had left for another city I visited them several times to find out how they were, and spent some time with them. My mother apologized to her Nazi brother in law. It didn't change him but it liberated her, she didn't live any more by reactions.

I traveled through most Western countries which had been occupied by Germany, and together with some friends asked for forgiveness. In general people responded warmly, and it was an uplifting experience.

A member of the group of Norwegians who invited us to their country was Leif Hovelsen. Leif was a member of the Norwegian resistance during the German occupation and spent nearly two years in a Gestapo prison in Oslo and in the Grini concentration camp, always close to death through execution. When the war ended and he was free again, he made a startling discovery. Leif came upon the hated commandant of the concentration camp together with his brutal special security officers, the men responsible for inflicting terror and suffering to thousands, in a group of prisoners of war disguised as air force officers.

He began to take his revenge and persecute these men as they had persecuted him and his fellow Norwegian prisoners. It did not satisfy him or make him feel any better, he realized that hatred and revenge are not only wrong, but will not cure any injustice. He apologized to the concentration camp commandant for his hatred. It was as difficult for him to apologize to a Nazi as it had been for my mother. This man, however, was a criminal and was later condemned to death for murder and executed. However, Leif had turned the key that opened the door to a free life.

One afternoon while in Trontheim, Norway, I was told that next day would be a national holiday, the Day of Liberation. I shuddered and thought that I better not show my face in the streets and stay in the home of my host. But it turned out that the liberation being commemorated was the one from Denmark a century earlier and not from the Germans. I was a cheerful participant in all of the events.

Then I visited Copenhagen and met quite a number of Danish people who showed us around, some had been in the Danish resistance against the Germans. I was together with an English friend, Brian, who was a mountain climber. All of a sudden we found ourselves in front of a memorial monument in honor of the men of the resistance who had been executed by the SS. Quite a number of wives, children, and parents of those killed were present.

On this occasion I found it very difficult to apologize and struggled terribly with a sense of pride and rebellion. Why should I always apologize, I thought, just because I was born a German? I had taken no part in what these execution commandos had done. I had never been in Denmark before. Brian, I argued within myself, can keep his head up while I have to take the blame. That is unfair I thought. I knew him inside out as he knew me. He was no better, and neither was I. Both of us were struggling with the same sins.

Then the better part in me took over, and I remembered that I was here because of the way I had insulted God and because my insults had helped make these Nazi crimes possible irrespective of what anybody else did or didn't do. I could then apologize to the families who had suffered with all my heart. They were warm-hearted, not bitter, received my words graciously, and then took me to dinner.

Making restitution to the Jewish people and striving for reconciliation between Germans and Jews is a priority in my heart and driving force in my life. To that end some years ago, twice, the then executive director of the Holocaust Memorial Center in Washington, Rabbi Dr. David Weinstein, received me. A member of the German Bundestag (Parliament), Peter Petersen, had set up the meeting for me. The encounter with Rabbi Weinstein was a deeply moving experience for both of us and he offered me his friendship. The event prompted me to pen these words for an American newspaper about the experience:

> The atrocity and inhumanity of the Holocaust was the extreme consequence of the arrogance of man, of human beings, who set themselves up above all others, despising the value of human life…I apologized to Rabbi Weinstein for the suffering Germany had inflicted on the Jewish people. I told him that the crimes of the Nazis were only possible because of the moral cowardice of so many of us non-Nazis. We Christians, the so-called good people, had a relative morality and only small goals.
>
> The opportunists outnumbered by far the men of the resistance who paid with their lives for opposing Hitler and his gang. Remembering the Holocaust, the focus should be on the bystanders and the appeasers of evil who were silent when faced at the beginning of the process with discrimination and injustice committed against others. It was not God who let the Holocaust happen. It was us who rejected His Commandments.
>
> My father died in a Soviet concentration camp no less inhuman then the Nazi camps. I have forgiven the Poles and the

Russians as I need forgiveness myself. If the suffering of millions of people is to have any meaning, it can only be the lesson that out of guilt and suffering, a spirit of forgiveness reconciliation, and common destiny can arise, leading in turn to the birth of a new human society where humanity obeys the laws of its creator. Before the Holocaust there was the evil spirit of hatred, class- and race-war, abuse of power, and despising of human life. My restitution for crimes committed by a German government in the name of Germany is the commitment of my life to fight this evil spirit in whatever form it appears in whatever part in the world so that the truth of God can be established who commands us to love our neighbors as ourselves.

When we remember the nightmare of those years with their repercussions throughout the whole world, proclaiming that we will never let it happen again, why then is it that the American and European governments, media and people are pathetically silent with regard to the Tibetan Holocaust? Communist China, a member of the Security Council of the United Nations, has been brutally and systematically attempting to eliminate a whole people and entire culture, murdering 1.3 million Tibetans, which represents a third of the population. That fact alone disqualifies the United Nations as a legitimate international institution.

No truthful person can deny the ruthless atrocity of the Holocaust. The German people and their leaders have faced the issue, I believe, and have been making restitution for it ever since. But to heal the pain of millions of people who suffered and to eradicate the attitudes which led to the Holocaust it needs a further step. You have to look for the motives of those who committed those crimes, of the bystanders, and the way evil escalated over few years. And then everybody has to learn how to change people.

CHAPTER EIGHT

THE NEXT THIRTY YEARS

I GRADUATED IN spring 1950 with satisfactory results from the University of Hamburg. Immediately afterwards I started to work with Moral Rearmament (MRA) first in Europe and later mostly in Latin America. I stayed with them nearly 20 years until 1969 when I left. The organization marshaled roughly 1,000 fulltime workers like me distributed on all continents, none of them receiving a salary.

We were not employees, instead, each of us followed his or her calling and we lived and worked by donations. Most of us felt the way I did: "Where God guides, He provides." The idea we fought for was to change the world based on God's moral absolutes expressed in the Ten Commandments and the condensed form of the Sermon on the Mount: absolute honesty, purity, unselfishness, and love.

I left the group because it had changed over time leading me to the conclusion that the inspiration and purpose, which moved me to invest my life in it to begin with, had disappeared. Replaced now by rules of behavior, and purposes that were mostly intellectual and not real or practical, in the end I wished I had left many years earlier.

But my thinking, which had begun from a global perspective, had been greatly influenced by Dr. Frank Buchman, the founder of MRA, and Peter Howard who died in Lima, Peru, where he had addressed the students of the San Marcus University. The American Frank Buchman was born and buried in Pennsylvania.

I worked with the Communist leaders of the labor union of the dockworkers in Rio de Janeiro, who came to realize that Communism with its concept of a classless society did not work in their own families, lived in a factory in Avellaneda, the industrial area of Buenos Aires, and spent a night in the Bolivian mining city of Siglo Veinte discussing justice with the Communist head of the local Mineworkers Union.

The mine had vertical shafts and some workers told me, that those who dared to oppose the powerful and corrupt union bosses were thrown down these shafts. The head of the national union, Juan Lechin, in later years a vice-president of Bolivia, kidnapped our international task force with our own special train. He wanted to blackmail the government but was unable hold us for a period of time long enough to achieve his objective.

All of those years are full of fascinating adventures and experiences. The most important exploit occurred on December 1, 1972, in Lima when I married the most beautiful girl in Peru, Dina Gamio Constantinides. I met her in a restaurant where the English fiancé of a Peruvian girl, a staff member at the headquarters of our international ADELA Investment Corporation, was "officially" dismissed from his status as a bachelor, Despedida de Soltero. I was the only executive invited for that dinner but had to decline since I already had accepted an invitation to another dinner party. But I agreed to come to the celebration following dinner.

In Lima after dinner meant close to midnight, and it was around that time that I arrived at the restaurant. There was a huge round table where our party was seated. On one side a number of people were sitting busily chattering, the other side was empty. A quick glance at the occupied side told me that there wasn't anybody of interest to me, so I sat down at the empty side.

Then I saw her returning from dancing—she was coming straight toward me. I had taken her seat. Looking at her, the first thing I said to myself was she is someone I could marry. The second thought was that she was probably too young for me. We said "Hola" to each other and the very first sentence I ever spoke to her was, "How old are you?" She told me. Well, I said inside to myself, it could just work out.

The staff member's wedding was next evening. Upon arriving at the church, another car came in from the other side and pulled up on my side. It was Dina! Together we entered the church and my girlfriend who was already seated in the church angrily watched when I sat down beside her. I have to admit that I didn't show my best side to the poor girl I was supposed to be with.

I took her home right after the end of the service, rushed back to the wedding party, and danced with Dina to my heart's delight. She always was an exciting person who liked traveling and had seen other countries. When I finally introduced her to my friends in Germany, some of them considered her exotic. For example, at that time there were only three girls in all of Peru who were skydivers. They had been trained by the air force and Dina was one of them. Nine months later we were married; it has been thirty-five years now. Dina not only is my wife but also part of our family team committed to changing the world that has involved a great deal of sacrifice on her part over the years and still does.

We are an international family. Our son Stefan was born in Jamaica and our daughter Sabrina in Mount Vernon, Ohio. They are Catholic while I am Lutheran. However, God's Commandments are the same for each one of us, and together we strive to integrate them deeply into American society and across the world. During the years we lived in Mexico we traveled with different passports. When we went skiing in Lake Tahoe, for instance, we flew via Los Angeles to Reno. When we passed through immigration I used to put Sabrina's American passport on top of my and Stefan's German and Dina's Peruvian passport. Then we sailed through the citizen entry which was much faster than the tourist entry. We had our fun with the officials who were always friendly and marveled at our international family composition. I always pointed out that Stefan was born in Jamaica and that our international family reflected a unity and level of cooperation that should have typified the United Nations but unfortunately was contrary to it.

Normal differences of opinions in my family often became amusing foreign policy issues. For example, Sabrina had realized early that she was something special. The rest of us had to deal with paperwork when we entered the U.S. but she did not. One Christmas Day we were visiting an Automobile Exhibition in Reno, Nevada, that filled three huge halls with different car models, old and new. Sabrina was around seven years old and still rather small. At the end of the last hall she saw some potato chips in a few vending machines resting against the wall, and told me that she wanted to eat some. I told her she could not have the chips since we were going to dinner shortly at the Christmas show in the MGM Hotel. Sabrina insisted and offered to pay for the potato chips herself pulling out a dollar bill I had given it to her earlier. When that didn't move me the persistent little diplomat promised that she would eat the potato chips after dinner. Again, I pointed out, "Whether you pay or I pay, whether you eat them before or after dinner, the effect will be the same, and you will not honor your expensive dinner I paid for. No potato chips!"

Her face grew red with anger and she looked up at me and said, "I am not going to look at these stupid cars anymore!" I tried to convince her that we might never come back here and that she should take advantage of this unique opportunity. "Never," she shot back at me, "when you are in Germany you can do as you please. Here in my country, in America, I do as I please, and I am not going to look at these stupid cars." She turned her back on me and stormed away. I didn't know what to say.

CHAPTER NINE

MEXICAN EXPERIENCES

THE GODLESS ESTABLISHMENT

AS A BUSINESSMAN in Mexico City I had to apply what I had learned during the process of digesting the Nazi years. The sheer godlessness with its consequent lack of character and failure to handle responsibility had to be answered by a quality of life which is attractive to the people I had to deal with. As a matter of fact, my recognition of my own nation's godlessness was tailor-made for Mexico. Godlessness is the principal problem of Mexico and the reason for the illegal presence of millions of Mexican workers in the United States.

The Institutional Revolutionary Party (PRI), for decades accustomed to rule as a one-party "democracy," had enforced a strict separation of church and state. This went so far that a member of the government was not allowed to enter a church. I remember very well that in one of my first years in Mexico the daughter of the President, Jose Lopes Portillo, got married. She was of course married in a Roman Catholic Church ceremony. But her father couldn't enter the church: he waited outside, and when the service was over and his daughter came out, he took her and her husband to the party that was waiting for them.

This policy was so strict that no religion could be taught at schools and priests were not even allowed to vote.

Since Catholicism in Latin-America has the tendency to be formal and is very often without substance, there is a great void of ethics in Mexican society. This was aggravated by the fact that all presidents I have known and their administrations down to the last police officer were a bunch of thieves who worked to fill their own pockets. That is the reason why millions of Mexicans in a country with rich resources and great beaches can't make a living. The search for a future for themselves and their families leads countless Mexicans to venture into the U.S. illegally. In other words, the Mexican government establishment first creates and maintains the overriding poverty of a great part of the Mexican population and then pushes the problem on to its wealthy neighbor.

Unfortunately, President Fox, the first conservative president, was part of the financial corruption. But just as I had to apologize for the crimes of a German government, in which I had no part, so must he and his successors face the real reason for the Mexican demise. And, once confronted, something fundamental must be done about it in Mexico, instead of pressuring President Bush and helping illegals to cross the border.

The first task of the Mexican government should be the creation of jobs. I am told that the oil production could be tripled from known resources in the Gulf of Mexico. There are also known reserves in Chiapas and Tabasco, oil and gas in Tampico. Mexico does not have the money and technology to tap these resources. They need foreign capital also for the secondary industries, like petrochemicals, aeronautics, nuclear energy, electricity and others. The national oil company, Petroleos Mexicanos (PEMEX) is a national idol as well as the heart of corruption. If the Mexican leadership is serious about solving the lack of jobs in their country and abstaining from creating a major problem for their neighbor in the north, then they need to find a way to get foreign capital in without losing the control of their national resources. Any American solution to the problem of the millions of illegal immigrants, most but not all people are desperate to get a job, should start with an assessment of how serious the Mexican government is to provide solutions within their own borders.

MY WORKFORCE

My experience with my Mexican workforce was rewarding. I was a supplier of the Volkswagen plant in Puebla and we produced push rod tubes for the air-cooled engine of the Beetle. It was the only Mexican factory to do so. When I entered the plant, Formamex, S.A. de C.V. for the first time as managing director I introduced myself, shook hands with everybody present, and asked for their cooperation. I kept the lines of communication open by informing them regularly of the perspectives of the company.

One of the many moral decisions I had made much earlier was to never step on others for my own advantage. So I said to myself that if the company did well, employees and workers should also do well. There is a law in Mexico, according to which every company must pay half a monthly salary to everybody on the payroll as a Christmas bonus. In my first year we did extremely well, prompting me to announce that instead of half, we would pay a full month's bonus, which we did on December 23. The week after Christmas we were scheduled to dispatch an export purchase order. When I came to the plant the day after Christmas nobody had reported for work. I was furious and listened to the laughter of the labor experts. Of course nobody would come having a double bonus in their pocket.

Next year was also a good year and again I announced that everybody would receive a bonus worth a whole month's salary. This time however, we paid half on December 23 and the other half on December 31. All workers came to work the week after Christmas. I congratulated myself. On the first work day following New Year nobody showed up. I was speechless. Mexico celebrates January 6 as Three Kings Day (Dia de los Reyes Magos), a day nearly as important as Christmas for the Latin-Americans and especially for the Mexican Catholics. On January 7 everybody showed up. Business as usual!

Another Christmas came along, and again we had a very good year. Just like the previous years I announced that we would pay a whole monthly salary extra. This time, however, we paid half a salary on December 23 and the other half some time after January 6. Everybody turned up on January 2. I had won. But so had they. In all my years with them I have never had a serious problem.

In the books of the Volkswagen plant we were Triple-A with an impeccable production rate and punctual delivery schedule. In 12 years we were subject to just one formal inspection from VW, though it was common for inspectors to constantly check the production of all their suppliers on a regular basis. The inspectors who scrutinized our factory saw how my workers operated and did not hesitate to tell me what difference it would make if they had the same spirit in their plant.

I had a great time with my workers and employees and we had many occasions for celebrating. We had mutual respect for each other and there was no class-war in my company. I had many arrangements in place like a doctor at hand if a worker or any of his immediate family got seriously ill; a monthly food basket, that made the wives happy, and a profit participation program on top of the Christmas Bonus. But above all I loved them as I loved myself and I understood their human quality. In December 2005, 15 years after I had sold the factory, I celebrated Christmas with quite a number of them. People of that caliber deserve an honest government and not a wishy-washy American policy.

THE THIEF WHO WAS MY PARTNER

I invited my best friend to take 25 percent of the capital of the company and to become the director of production. That was about the dumbest decision I ever made and an expression of my severely miss-reading the character of someone close to me. He once had told me that everybody he met he would use him to get richer. I hadn't taken that seriously. Their children went to school with our children and our families spent lots of time together. My agreement with my friend, a German-Columbian, was that he would make me a partner of one of his companies the same way I had taken him into my company. It never happened. Furthermore he paid very little of his 25 percent of the capital, most of it came out of the company itself. I was very naïve, but costly lessons are well learned.

He had a factory that produced medical instruments right next to ours and drove a hole through the wall of my factory to connect his operations with our electrical services. In other words, our company paid his factory's electric bill. Additionally, he would show up at our plant with a non-company car, load it with boxes containing 200 of our push-rod tubes and sell them on the black market. He threatened our two supervisors with termination if they said a word to me. He had already terminated our production manager and the plant secretary lying to me about why it was necessary. Sadly, I discovered that he was using me and had planned to cheat me from the very beginning.

As if that wasn't brazen enough, he began to try to get rid of me. Our technology partner, the HeidemannWerke in Einbeck, Germany, could swing the management and go with me or with him. They were decent people and stayed with me sending me all the communications between them and our dubious partner. He also tried to tarnish my good name by lying about me in a highly indecent manner.

There was another legal twist in his favor, which could have made my life miserable, and where our lawyer, a Mexican general and a friend of his, could have done me great harm. My partner held my part of the company's equity in a trust arrangement that could have had serious repercussions. Thankfully, the lawyer had also become a friend of mine and was honest enough not to go along with his schemes, electing to stick to the correct legal procedures. It was a tenuous battle that lasted several months where I was never far from losing everything. If my former best friend succeeded in ousting me, I would have been destitute, on the street with my family and small children with no money, in a country that was not my own, without a work permit (which was linked to the factory), and with nowhere to go.

At the end there was an arrangement through a friend of mine by which he could keep the real estate company, which owned the land and the factory building. I had named the real estate company after my wife, Dina. He had no rights to it but apparently had bribed a judge and my lawyers. I kept the factory and had to pay rent but as long as I paid it he couldn't throw me out.

It didn't take long for him to make his move. My "friend" arrived with a court order and moving equipment, and threw all my machines on the street. To make matters worse, the heavens opened and rain fell in buckets on my machinery. The justification for him to do this was that the rent had not been paid. My rent checks were written faithfully each month, but the money never arrived where it should have. I had retained a new attorney who was to take the rent check each month and deposit it to assure that there would be no problems. I shouldn't have been, but I was shocked to discover that instead of paying my rent, he kept the money for himself. In retrospect I have to believe that he was probably bribed as well.

I heard about what happened to my machines in Colorado Springs when I was just leaving for the airport to catch a plane to Germany. I was in the middle of negotiations to sell the company and now did not even know if I had a factory to sell. I could not do anything about my machinery; it would be on the street before I could get there even if I now flew to Mexico. However, I could try to assure that I would not lose my buyer so I decided to trust my people and fly to Germany.

In my absence, all my workers and employees toiled late into the night and saved the machines. They moved them into the warehouse of a friend who offered me the space shortly before my plane left the airport. And I was able to sell the company shortly afterwards thanks to the heroic efforts of my workers and employees. Our family had to struggle through some agonizing months, however, because the buyers, who were Brazilian, didn't pay up. When they finally came through with the major part of their debt to me, I was free to embark on new ventures—at an age when most people retire.

When God liberated our family from hatred and I had learned about its devastating power, I made a decision that I would never again allow anybody to pull me down so low that I would hate him for whatever they did to me. Even though this German/Columbian had brought me and my family close to annihilation, I kept my promise to God. I remained free of resentment and hatred, and trusted the Lord to show me a new road—which He did! Again it was a ruthless liar whose lies had threatened our survival.

My Prime Client

The Mexican Volkswagen plant usually bought about 40 percent of my production, 35 percent was allocated to the national spare part market and the remaining 25 percent was exported to the United States. Volkswagen had a policy that their suppliers were required to explain their costs to them in order to justify a price hike. Since we had to deal sometimes with a yearly inflation rate of about 150 percent all the suppliers were forced to raise prices repeatedly.

A fellow supplier once told me, that we could not survive if we were honest. He was referring to the normal praxis of suppliers, namely to state their costs at 130 percent in order to get the 100 percent they wanted and needed. With that dishonest calculation they then went to the bargaining table, discussed, groaned, threw their hands up and normally got somewhat more than they needed. The Volkswagen buyer felt satisfied because he had brought the price of the supplier down and the supplier smiled to himself because he got what he wanted and swindled Volkswagen.

I did not like the idea of lying to my principal client and basing our relationship on deception. Neither did I like the idea of allowing another company, as big as it was, to try to control my costs. When the time came for me to raise my prices I went to the VW plant in Puebla without cost calculation and waited in the conference room for the buyer assigned to Formamex to come in. On this occasion, the purchasing employee walked in, accompanied by a young assistant. Very friendly he offered me coffee, which I accepted. I proceeded to say: "You know, with this inflation we simply cannot maintain our prices. I get my steel from the Krupp factory in Germany and the price of the Deutsch-Mark in Pesos is constantly rising. Prices for about everything in Mexico are continuously going up as well." I proceeded to explain that, due to these circumstances, I had been forced to raise my prices, and that from the next month on the price would be such and such.

He remained friendly and asked to see my cost calculation. I told him that I did not have my calculation with me, but that I had given him a fair price. It took him some time to realize that I was serious and had no intention of giving him a calculation. All of a sudden his whole attitude changed. He was barking at me telling me how ignorant I was, and how it could be possible that I was rejecting his friendly offer to help me to get the best price acceptable to both of us. I answered that no help was needed as I was perfectly capable of looking after my own company. I also suggested that he should do the same with his.

At this point, the climate in the room grew extremely tense due to the way he shouted at me. I didn't say anything and he stormed out of the room with the embarrassed assistant leaving shortly afterwards. During my two-hour drive back to Mexico City I became gravely concerned and asked myself whether I was crazy for having provoked such a crisis. "What will happen if I lose this client?" I thought. The company would not be viable any more. They could very easily decide to buy their tubes in Brazil or in Germany.

By the time I arrived at my office, I had come to the conclusion that attack is the best defense. I fired off a letter of protest to the management of Volkswagen complaining about the bad treatment by an employee of their company towards an independent company owner and supplier. Back at that time in Mexico City these kinds of letters were sent by messengers. They answered me, I answered back, and in the end they accepted my position. Never again was I asked for my cost calculation. The Volkswagen management was fair, I gained their respect, and I never abused them. I asked only for what was justified by the inflation, which they knew. And I must also admit that they were in a difficult position having to deal with who they well knew were many dishonest people. They simply couldn't allow the prices to go through the roof if they wanted to stay in business. The same is true for the leaders of the company today as well as for future managment.

MY FAMILY

My son Stefan was born in Jamaica where I had my office as regional managing director of the Caribbean area for my company ADELA. I was on the telephone with my midwife sister Sibylle in Ohio constantly monitoring every movement of the developing birth. She tranquillized me. Everything unfolded normally and suddenly Dina and I had a son. From the very beginning Dina spoke to him in Spanish while I spoke to him in German. English was all around us so we focused on our native languages. Sixteen months later Sabrina was born in Ohio. We were in the middle of pulling out of Jamaica and Dina stayed with my sister. We took the same approach to languages, with Sabrina but then moved into Mexico where I was a minority. To continue teaching our children the English and German languages we sent them to my sister during their vacations, first to Ohio and then Mississippi.

But we also went to Europe nearly every summer. Once I left Dina with friends in Bremen located in North Germany, Sabrina with a friend in West Germany, and Stefan with friends in South Germany. They couldn't talk to each other in Spanish and were forced several weeks to try to communicate in German. Everybody suffered except me. But because of these kind of exercises Stefan, Sabrina, and Dina became tri-lingual. It makes a lot of difference in life for you not only learn the languages but also learn to appreciate different cultures. Other nations and what makes them tick have been part of our family from its onset and we have friends in many parts of the world.

We bought a horse for Stefan. He named it Moby Dick. It didn't take long and we spent one weekend after the other at the different show places mostly in Mexico City. Stefan won many shows. He is the 1989 Mexican Junior National Champion (Champion Nacional de Salto de obstaculos). Sabrina became an ice skater, and Dina and I had to get her to the ice rinks and to her competitions. Both Stefan and Sabrina were also outstanding athletes and won many championships in their school competitions and Stefan on horse shows and as captain of the Idaho State University's Track Team.

RESUME

As one person among millions, the course of my routine life brought me face to face with the most destructive forces within our society: greed, hatred, and indifference. I was in the middle of the same godlessness that had destroyed Germany and our family. It was simply repackaged: greed guided my dishonest partner as well as the government system. Hatred can quickly enter a human heart but I kept my promise to God and refused to allow myself to be dominated by the desire for revenge, fighting a clean battle. I had found the answer to hatred and greed in my heart when I faced my moral responsibility for the Nazi disaster.

Human nature is the same in all parts of the world. In one way or the other everybody has to face his own nature and the destructive forces in and around him. We can all clean up our lives and find new motives and a new purpose. I have become firmly convinced that everybody can make a difference in whatever situation he or she finds him- or herself, have a part in healing what is wrong in our society, and change the world. That is what our politicians pretend to aim at but they forget that their own moral change must come first.

Changing the world for our family is not a theoretical proposition:

it became a practical task, which, however, had to be paid for. After having worked 20 years with Moral Rearmament without earning a cent, I made good money after I left it. According to my auditor and my own calculations, I have thus far invested considerably more than one million U.S. dollars in the battle for the truth of God out of my own pocket. My and my family's lives would be much easier if we had kept those funds for ourselves. Several times I faced disaster, death or financial annihilation. Some of those experiences I have mentioned in this book. God never let me and my family down and always opened a new door. All that I have, including myself, is His. And there must be another door which needs to open now.

CHAPTER TEN

THE REAL NEO-NAZIS

DEFINITION OF A NEO-NAZI

PEOPLE AND NATIONS who are committed to or are part of an ideology of hatred which climbs on the backs of other people to seize world power, are godless and inside no different from the Nazis. Their ideologies are godless and they don't respect life and family. They are the real Neo-Nazis who carry the anti-God destructive Nazi spirit across the globe. The idea that some punks, who paint a swastika on some walls, represent the Neo-Nazis in Germany is laughable. They are just punks. The socialist/green government coalition, who held the reins of power for many years in Germany, comes much closer to the definition. They are fellow socialists of the Nazis. Leaders of nations, who tolerate, finance, or aid terrorism, which means the murder of innocent people, are true Neo-Nazis and are without what the Bible calls true religion.

Neo-Nazis are being joined and helped by those who deny God through the way they live. It is not by accident that a great many of the anti-American slogans circulating in the globe today are being created by Americans in America, who may go to church like the German Nazi 'Christians' did. They are nevertheless godless even if they sit in pews and sing hymns each Sunday morning. The common factor for the global anti-God alliance which today normally includes anti-Americanism is a set of lies as I tried to explain at the beginning of this book with my own experience, which made me and Germany instruments of Hitler and the Nazi agenda. All godlessness is based on lies like the concept that a woman has the right to kill an unborn human being. The ideological organization of lies and hatred on a global scale, based on the ignorance of what is right and wrong, has now reached a stage that threatens the life and freedom of every last person in the world.

There is no way to solve humanity's problems without God, the Creator of all. And this is not a personal religious opinion, but the reality of this world. The Nazis could only exercise their evil deeds because of the millions of bystanders who were mostly concerned with themselves and loved safety more than what was right. What I am saying is that just as then, in today's environment, nobody—and especially no Christian—can be a neutral bystander in the face of the assault on God and His Commandments. Our civilization will otherwise be destroyed.

This sentence is directed at the 300,000 American pastors the majority of whom refuse to enter the battle for national moral issues and the spiritual resurrection of this nation. If they did, they could change the situation immediately because there is still more moral substance in America than in any other nation.

THE LACK OF UNDERSTANDING IDEOLOGY

No political leader will be able to do an adequate job in the contemporary world unless he understands the nature of an ideology. If American leaders would understand it, our society would be quite different and much closer to our Constitution. If they understand the underlying reality of the Nazi ideology they also would understand the workings of Marxism/Socialism/Communism as well as the nature of Terrorism. Additionally, they would realize what to do about it.

These seemingly different philosophies, including the philosophy of the so-called "moderate" Social-democrats, Republicans, and Liberals, are morbid fruits from the same poisonous tree. And unless we uproot that tree vs. just going after individual branches there will be no justice or peace, ever. The *idea* of freedom, not defined precisely, is no match for a militant materialistic *ideology*. You can beat a bad ideology only with a better one. In our case: the idea of freedom will die if not raised to the ideology of freedom which demands everything from a person, career, money, reputation, existence, and a life based on absolute moral standards.

Western people have to match the level of engagement of the suicide terrorists who give their lives for a purpose greater than self. Young people are especially hungry for such a purpose especially if they are promised sex in heaven. Our soldiers in Iraq who put their lives on the line to bring freedom to others have a purpose bigger than self. But it ends when they come back since our society cannot integrate this purpose into everyday life. There is no challenge. The Christian message has become a purely personal matter and you strive simply to get to heaven. To make money is the other personal incentive, which if it stands alone, ends in corruption.

John Negroponte, the director of national intelligence, stated according to Bill Gertz at the beginning of 2006 in an annual intelligence threat briefing for Congress "that China's rise is similar to that of democratic India." He left out any reference to the threat to Asia and the United States posed by the extraordinary Chinese military buildup. In April of 2007 he played down the nuclear threat of Iran. This man doesn't know what he is talking about and he is a danger to America if policy makers base their policy decisions on his distorted views.

The Quadrennial Defense Report published by the Defense Department two weeks before his briefing gets closer to the truth by defining China as the greatest potential challenge to the US military. But the report is also incomplete because it does not spell out the purpose and the nature of the Chinese Communist government. It talks about the U.S. goal to help China pursue peaceful economic development and political liberalization. This does not exist in China and will never exist as long as there is a Communist government. But they are more than willing to take advantage of our naivety. Any Communist government is committed to world revolution aiming at a Socialist world order.

Their motives are guided by a global ideology of hatred—as were Hitler and the Nazi establishment. They and their followers believe themselves to be part of a history making purpose.

Journalist Brigitte Gabriel, founder of the American Congress of Truth, in a speech at the Intelligence Summit in Washington, DC, on February 18, 2006, referring to the war on terrorism, clearly defined what we must begin with: "The most important element of intelligence has to be the understanding of the mindset and intention of the enemy. The West has been wallowing in a state of ignorance and denial for thirty years...America cannot effectively defend itself in this war unless the American people understand the nature of the enemy we face."

And what is it that we face? We are up against different mindsets with different ideological reasoning, but all coming from the same amoral godless root. Those promoting these ideologies would float any lies to deceive the naïve Western World and its leaders. They strive to conceal their real purpose and think nothing of killing at random.

"The ideological challenge that the Jihadists are making to the West remains the single most misunderstood aspect of the war on Terror," writes Robert Spencer in his new book *Religion of Peace?* a review of which was published by the weekly *Human Events*. "Since Islam is a political and social system as well as a religious faith, to accept it is not merely to change one's religious affiliation—it would fundamentally alter the nature of Western society."

"Six years after 9/11, and a year and a half after Donald Rumsfeld observed that 'we need to find ways to win the ideological battle as well' the Jihadists' ideological challenge [to embrace Islam] is not being answered adequately. Osama's challenge to Christianity and advocacy of Sharia is an opportunity for Western leaders to stress the aspects of Judeo-Christian civilization that Sharia law denies—notably the equality of dignity of men and women and the freedom of conscience. But no Western leader will do this, because it would contradict the multi-cultural dogma that no civilization or culture has any virtues that others do not possess."

Our political leaders, however, start in this conflict as in most others on the wrong footing, denying our cultural and traditional roots based on our unique Constitution and Christian orientation as a nation. Christians don't understand their mission.

American analysts, including John Negroponte, are either covertly part of one of the mentioned ideologies or understand ideology as little as the British and French heads of government. Neville Chamberlain and Edouard Daladier (respectively), understood the Nazi ideology when they dealt with Hitler in 1938. When they thought that they had secured "peace for all times" they had in reality opened the direct road to World War II. Hitler had long before decided to go to war and lied to them about his intentions. If they had read his book *Mein Kampf,* and had taken it seriously, they probably would not have fooled themselves as they did.

The same is true for modern day politicians. Most of them have neither studied Marxism/Leninism nor Islam I suspect. They are like blind people driving a race car in which we, the people, sit. They are constantly outmaneuvered, and are not aware of it. The United States has more enemies than friends in the world, but the truly deadly enemies are not being identified as such by our leaders.

An ideology consists of a philosophy, a purpose, and a plan, and needs people who are committed with their life to implement the plan and make the purpose reality. Power is the name of the game and not democracy or economic growth. The economy is just necessary for carrying the ideology forward.

America has the philosophy and a prescribed purpose but lacks an ideology. The idea of freedom is totally insufficient because it is not properly defined and presented. For many it only means "I can do as I please." Similarly, Christianity today has no ideology. It has adjusted its message to the comfortable and sinful lifestyle of the present generation, just as many Germans adjusted Christian teachings to the Nazi ideology and presented themselves as Christians. Many Latin Americans get fooled by the Communist Theology of Liberation which used similar tactics. Godless ideologists present themselves as priests and infect people with a class warfare ideology. The Jesuit priest Olivero Medina, for instance, came 2002 as ambassador for the rebel "Columbian Revolutionary Armed Forces" to Brazil and delivered money from Hugo Chavez to the then president of the Communist Workers Party Luis Inacio Lula da Silva for his campaign for the presidency of Brazil.

There is a similar approach to Africans and African Americans. The senior pastor at the Trinity United Church of Christ in Chicago, the Rev. Dr. Jeremiah A. Wright Jr. explained his theology according to an article from Ron Strom, published on January 9, 2008 in *WorldNetDaily* "…it is based upon the systemized liberation theology that started 1969 with the publication of Dr. James Cone's book, 'Black Power and Black Theology.'" He explains on his Web site that he has a church whose theological perspective starts from the vantage point of black liberation theology.

The Black Theology, however, is not the beginning of the theology of liberation. It is a local version of the Latin American original which is aimed at Catholic Latins but aimed at Africans and African Americans. There are other versions aimed at American Natives, Asians and Women.

In my first book which was published 1989 in Germany I have a whole chapter on this theology. I had visited the founder of the liberation theology, the Peruvian priest Gustavo Gutierrez in his home in Lima, had read their literature and listened to their leaders like the Brazilian Franciscan priest Leonardo Boff, and discussed in UNAM, the state university in Mexico, with the theology professor Johann B. Metz. The general motto is: "Christian love only is a historical force if it takes up class warfare."

Barack Hussein Obama has been a member of the Rev. Wright's church for 20 years. I find it doubtful that he as a highly intelligent person has not become aware in those years of the orientation of his church. Liberation theology is a subversive political movement, promotes Marxism with Christian vocabulary and tries to destroy America's moral foundation. Most likely Obama is part of an international radical Socialist anti-Christian and anti free-society network which presents itself as Christian similar to the "German Christians." The programs he promotes in the 2008 presidential election campaign are Marxist and anti-American. Since, furthermore, abortion is part of his political program he is not a Christian but a fake Christian. He should not be president.

I cannot go into the details of the liberation theology in the framework of this book. There is plenty of information in the internet for anybody who wants to know more.

The National Socialist (Nazi) ideology had the same purpose as the Socialist Marxist/Leninist ideology: world power. The United Nations is on the same track. Today the one obstacle on the road to that power is the United States of America. Therefore, China and Soviet Russia work hand in hand to destroy that obstacle while the U.S. does not seem to notice. Independent of each other they and the American ideologists of godlessness and immorality nevertheless work together because they are out to destroy the moral fiber of this nation. America needs a God-centered ideology to prevail! I shall come to it at the end of this book.

In America, people speak of "Nazism," a ridiculous description which didn't exist in Nazi Germany, and call it "Fascism" but not National *Socialism* and that is where our ideological self-deception begins.

THE SOVIET STRATEGY

Even though the Soviets came to power 15 years before the Nazis I list them under Neo-Nazis because of their close ideological link and common godlessness. They belong at the top of the list.

On March 26 of 1987 the Soviet Politburo made a decision on the USSR's future policy toward Western Europe. President Gorbachev who was also secretary general of the Communist Party formulated the gist of this policy which sounded like a battle order: *To Strangle in Embrace.*

It means to embrace America as a fellow democrat and then destroy it. According to well-known former Soviet Dissident Vladimir Bukovsky, who managed to get access to a number of top classified documents including reports by the KGB to the Politburo, this concept had already a specific name in the inner circle of the Soviet leadership—"Common European Home." Lenin coined this phrase at the beginning of the twenties as a possible step for taking control of Europe.

At that Politburo meeting "Common European Home" was given highest priority. Gorbachev strictly prohibited making any political decisions without considering it. In his own words the policy included not splitting Western Europe from the U.S.A. but instead, ousting the U.S.A. from Europe. The structure and the Constitution of the European Community are by Soviet design with the added godlessness of the French revolution. Conversely, while I haven't heard any president stating it recently, the structure and the Constitution of the United States include God by design and are based on the Bible.

Most of Europe's Socialist leaders but also "Conservatives" like Giscard D'Estaing from France and John Major of Britain, Hans-Dietrich Genscher, German foreign minister and head of the fiscally conservative FDP Party, either went to Moscu or met with Gorbachev elsewhere to discuss how to proceed. Genscher's KGB code name according to author Christopher Story was "Tulpe" and he was controlled for years by chief Soviet controller of agents of influence, Aleksandre Bessmertnykh.

Among the Socialist Leaders were Francois Mitterand, former President of France, Willy Brandt, former German chancellor and Chairman of the Socialist International, J. Delors, Chairman of the Commission of the European Communities, G. Berthoin, Co-Chairman of the Trilateral Commission, Henry Kissinger, and many others. The Socialists came to get Gorbachev's advice if not instructions on how to create a Socialist Europe. "The success of perestroika means only one thing" stated the Spanish Foreign Minister F. Fernandez Ordonez to Gorbachev, "the success of the socialist revolution in contemporary conditions of the world community." Gorbachev answered him, "Today we, the communists, are working to realize the potential of socialism as fully as possible through perestroika."

In America he of course speaks a different language. With a pious face I saw him speak about Jesus Christ in a well-known church in California. The pastor and his applauding congregation are fools and unable to see through this charade. The Communist Gorbachev is atheist and his purpose is to merge American and Soviet societies on his conditions in order for socialism to consume America from within. Christians in the meanwhile are concerned with getting to heaven.

"The substance of the directives under which we operate is that we shall use our grant-making power to alter life in the United States so that we comfortably merge with the Soviet Union," explained the president of the Ford Foundation, Rowan Gaither, in 1953 to Norman Dodd, Staff Director of the Congressional Committee to Investigate Tax Exempt Foundations, known as the Reece Committee in recognition of its chairman, Congressman Carroll Reece. Dodd had overwhelming evidence that the vast wealth of the foundations was being funneled into activities that promoted a Socialist anti-American worldview. He was not allowed to continue his investigation. I have no reason not to assume that the Ford Foundation's policy is still the same.

The political and ideological reality of today is that the Communist Party of the Soviet Union is operating underground and controls developments in Russia as well as in most of the "new democratic" states of the former Soviet Union. There are only few or no "former" Communists in the Russian Duma—they are all trained Communists and part of the charade developed teaming up with Gorbachev, Jelzin, Putin, and the Central Committee of the Communist Party. Designed to pull wool over the eyes of the world, especially of the American leadership, the purpose is a tactical one: to merge Russia with Western societies on an equal footing on Russia's conditions. Gorbachev's words are haunting, "embrace and strangle." It was and is a highly successful operation described by Christopher Story with plenty of inside information on how it was and is being done in his book, *The European Union Collective—Enemy of its Member States.*

The wife of well known dissident Andrei Sakharov explained, "The point is that the Communist goal is fixed and changeless—it never varies one iota from their objective of world domination, but if we judge them only by the direction in which they *seem* to be going, we shall be deceived."

To believe that that purpose fundamentally changes transforming a Communist into a democrat is beyond naïve. It is a suicidal expression similar to the wishful thinking that guided Chamberlain and Daladier in their dealings with Hitler or guided the West in trying to make Hamas and the corrupt Palestine Authority partners for peace. Another defector, Tomas Schuman, who lives in the United States, used to say, that "the Soviet system is an elaborate maze of compulsive lies. We cheat everywhere, on any occasion, through all ages, and for a variety of purposes, or without any."

It is nearly incredible that this clever attack on our nation and our freedom, carried out by hundred thousands of apparatchiks in a dozen countries, and continuing for nearly twenty years has never been defined by the CIA and all the many other intelligence services. Are they incompetent or just taken over by anti-American Soviet moles? Our leadership doesn't know what they are up against and doesn't understand the mindset of their enemies. I very much doubt that George W. Bush saw Putin's soul when he looked into his eyes as he reported to the world. Putin is KGB and neither Bush's nor America's friend and as such, he should have no access to Western institutions, like NATO.

On this sole compound lie that "the Soviet Union has fallen" and "Communism and the USSR has collapsed" the next lie was built—that the threat derived from Communist aggression and expansion has vanished. Christopher Story said it best when he wrote that it was the "image of the enemy that was being destroyed *rather than the enemy itself.*" Lenin had taught his disciples Communist morality the substance of which is to lie incessantly for the Revolution and that everything which furthers the revolution is moral. He stated, "We must be ready to employ trickery, deceit, law-breaking, withholding and concealing truth. We can and must write in the language which sows among the masses hate, revulsion, scorn, and the like, toward those who disagree with us."

The problem is that politicians have not studied Marxism/Leninism and have never seen this quote and similar ones. They live by wishful thinking.

Anatoly Golitsyn, former officer in the counter-intelligence section of the KGB who defected in 1961 and is now an American citizen, has warned the CIA and other Western intelligence services for more than 40 years about Soviet intentions. He laid it out in his books *New Lies for Old* and *The Perestroika Deception* but nevertheless the deception continues and U.S. foreign policy ignores the reality. "Gorbachev," he wrote, is "a Leninist, chosen and trained by the Soviet strategists to engineer the defeat of the United States and the West generally through the use of a false, controlled democracy and a specious capitalism."

Leninists are ruthless opportunists and criminals of the worst kind. They are in their disregard of other people's rights and lives like the Nazis—only better organized and much more intelligent than their fellow totalitarian Socialists.

Having faced the truth of God for Germany and myself as I described earlier in this book, I then learned to apply that standard to everybody. In my life, there remained not one trespass or any damage I had inflicted on others of which I was conscious that I did not put right before God and those I hurt. I traveled around Europe and to Israel to ask forgiveness from our neighbors and Jews for the crimes of my government even though I had not personally committed any of them. When I saw that neither Gorbachev nor Putin, nor any of the Soviet leaders recognized the moral perversion of their philosophy or the crimes the Soviet Union, the Communist Party, and their armies had committed and refused to apologize for anything, it was clear to me that none of them had changed. I have known for a long time that they are dangerous gangsters, imposters, pseudo-democrats, and that the politicians and Christians who take their words at face value and dream that we have won the cold war better face the truth of God in their own life before they make political decisions.

Soviet strategy is global and each local piece of tactics, which can change overnight, is part of it. Soviet Union founder Vladimir Ilyich Lenin put down the final goal for all Communists: Global power. That purpose is the same today as nearly a hundred years ago and never changes. Since American politicians live in the first place for their re-elections—and European are not very different—they don't understand what they are up against. Their ridiculous political and economic reasoning only opens the door to moral subversion, which is the road to the global totalitarian system they want.

"Today's international terrorism was conceived at the Lubyanka, the headquarters of the KGB, in the aftermath of the 1967 Six-day War in the Middle East" states Rumanian Lt. General Ion Mihai Pacepa in his article "Russian Footprints," which was published by the *NationalReviewOnline* on August 24, 2006. Pacepa is the former chief of the DIE, then Rumanian equivalent of the CIA or KGB, who defected 1978 to the West and is now an American citizen. He is author of the book *Red Horizons.*

"I witnessed its birth in my other life as a Communist general. Israel humiliated Egypt and Syria, whose bellicose governments were being run by Soviet razvedka (Russian for 'foreign intelligence') advisers, whereupon the Kremlin decided to arm Israel's enemy neighbors, the Palestinians, and draw them into a terrorist war against Israel."

"General Aleksandr Sakharovsky, who created Communist Rumania's intelligence structure and then rose to head up all of Soviet Russia's foreign intelligence, often lectured me, 'In today's world, when nuclear arms have made military force obsolete, terrorism should be our main weapon.'"

"In 1972, the Kremlin decided to turn the whole Islamic world against Israel and the U.S. As KGB Chairman Yuri Andropov told me, a billion adversaries could inflict far greater damage on America than could a few millions. We needed to instill a Nazi-style hatred for the Jews throughout the Islamic world, and to turn this weapon of the emotions into a terrorist bloodbath against Israel and its main supporter, the United States. No one within the American/Zionist sphere of influence should any longer feel safe."

I have read the writings of Pacepa, of Major General Jan Sejna, a former member of the Czechoslovakian Central Committee of the Communist Party, a member of Parliament and its presidium, first party secretary at the ministry of defense (where he was also chief of staff) and a member of the Minister's Colegium. He was also secretary of the Defense Council, the top decision-making body in matters of defense, foreign policy, intelligence, and economy. He was a central player in the establishment of the structures for the unfolding drug war and represented Czechoslovakia in the meetings with the Soviet Security Council. He defected in 1968 and lived in the United States but was never debriefed by the CIA.

I also met in Buenos Aires Eudocio Ravines and read his book *The Yennan Way*. He was the founder of the Communist Party of Peru, a Latin American delegate to the Communist International in Moscow where he was trained by Mao Tse Tung for the power struggle. Stalin ordered him to make Chile a Socialist country. He left the Communist party when Stalin made a pact with Hitler realizing that he had misjudged Stalin and Communism. He was killed by a car in a traffic accident in Mexico City.

Earlier in this book I wrote about Vladimir Bukovsky. Each one of these men, and there is a myriad of others with a similar backgrounds, have described in detail how our deadly enemies go about to defeat us. It makes absolutely no difference to American policy makers. On the contrary, now we have a presidential candidate who thinks he can talk our enemies into friends and partners. I warn Americans, if we don't deal with the self-absorbed ignorants in Washington they are capable of leading us into self-destruction. If Obama thinks that way he is most likely in his ideology closer to our enemies than to our founding Fathers. In America of today unfortunately he is not alone.

THE CHINESE UNRESTRICTED WARFARE

The Chinese Colonels Qiao Liang and Wang Xiangsui made it clear in their book *Unrestricted Warfare* how relativism will determine all future wars. "The first rule in this warfare," they state, "is that there are no rules. Everything is allowed, nothing is forbidden." They express the mindset of Chinese military strategists. The battlefield can be anywhere; anything can be used as a weapon and there is no difference between soldiers and civilians. The Islamic terrorists already practice this approach. According to the Chinese, however, victory can be achieved not necessarily by killing the enemy, but by lying to him in order to control him. Where have I heard that before? That is exactly what the Nazis did. With their lies they persuaded us to decide of our own volition, to do what they wanted us to. Why kill somebody when you get someone else to do the job for you by an act of their free will, when you can use them? You only kill them when they refuse to be manipulated.

The Chinese Communists are partners of Soviet Russia in their quest for world power. They arm and train our enemies like North Korea, Syria, Venezuela, and Iran. They are as ruthless as the Nazis and pose a growing major military threat to America. By the end of 2005 "China had deployed some 710–790 mobile CSS-7 short-range ballistic missiles to garrisons opposite Taiwan. SRBM deployment continues to expand at an average rate of about 100 missiles per year. Newer versions feature improved range and accuracy," states Howard Phillips in his intelligence letter HPISP 794. "China has more than 700 combat aircraft based within unrefueled operational range of Taiwan and the airfield capacity to expand the aircraft within this range. China has 400,000 ground forces personnel deployed in three military regions opposite Taiwan, an increase of 25,000 over last year. China has been upgrading these units with tanks, armored personnel carriers and a substantial increase in the amount of artillery pieces. China's military expansion is already such as to alter regional military balances…the Chinese continue to upgrade their missile system, which now include the "extended-range DF-31A, which can target most of the world, including the continental United States."

China has become a military, economic, and financial force to reckon with. Holding at the beginning of August 2007 US $1.33 trillion in their monetary reserves China is able among other things to inflict great damage to our financial infrastructure. They use their financial power strategically with the ultimate purpose of isolating and destroying us. Add to that the intentions of some of the oil producers like Venezuela and Iran to substitute the dollar currency with the Euro for payment for oil and the threat to our very existence should become clear to anybody who thinks. Are we a free nation when the Chinese with their money and the Arabs and oil producers can strangle us?

China is also developing the technological know-how for damaging American military Satellites. According to Lieutenant General Kevin Campbell, head of US Army's Space and Missile Defense Command, this is a most dangerous threat to the United States communication system denying the military access to space on which they depend in the case of war. They also seem capable of hacking computers in key areas of Western governments. China's aggressive spying, technology theft and computer attacks pose most significant threats to U.S. national security officials and analyst told a congressional hearing on January 29, 2008, reported the *Washington Times*.

TimesOnline reported on August 6, 2007, the beginning of joint military exercises of Russian and Chinese troops and aircraft in the Chelybinsk region of Russia. Tajikistan, Kyrgyzstan, Kazakhstan, and Uzbekistan were also involved in the military project. Called "Peace Mission 2007," these are the first international maneuvers of this kind and therefore some American military analysts are considering the participating nations as a potential rival to NATO.

I recently heard presidential candidate Barak Obama tell his audience that he doesn't think that China is an enemy. Instead, he characterized the nation in more benign terms saying, "it is a competitor." I say that he doesn't know what he is talking about—or does he? Heaven help us if he comes to lead this nation. His concepts are as unreal as the statement of Nancy Pelosi after her visit to Damascus that "the road to peace goes through Syria."

China is supposed to host the 2008 Olympic Games. The Committee (which decided to apply what I call the Bush doctrine—embrace your Socialist enemies, be nice to them and include them in what you do) had obviously forgotten the 1936 Olympic Games in Berlin. They were a huge success for Hitler who became the savior of the nation in the eyes of millions of Germans. The resulting public relations bonanza paralyzed the then emerging military resistance which would get no backing from the population for a coup against Hitler. Therefore they didn't try.

Mind control is the decisive difference between a totalitarian regime and any other form of government. Under totalitarian rule, a person doesn't realize that he or she is being controlled, instead thinking that the conclusions they reach in a given set of circumstances are their own. Inadvertently, they freely do what the regime wants them to do, a ploy that I and millions of others who went to war fell for believing that we were defending our country.

Similarly, China is a totalitarian society driven by a government which persecutes those whose thinking is different from theirs. Christians, as well as adherents to all religions, are being persecuted by their Communist government. It is estimated that there are 82 million Christians—much more than the 65 million members of the Communist Party. Is the message of the United States and the other Western nations to the Chinese people that we are friends with their slave masters?

Mind control was not invented by the Nazis. The Soviet Union was the first state to exploit it and Putin is busy in Russia cultivating it again. The Communist government of China established the system at the very beginning of its rule and according to the August 12, 2007 of the New York Times, is expanding it by installing surveillance cameras throughout the city of Shenzhen with 12.4 million inhabitants.

The Times reported that every inhabitant receives a residence card fitted with powerful computer chips that contain names and addresses, work history, educational background, the telephone number of their landlord, religion, police record, medical insurance status, ethnicity, and personal reproductive activity. The latter enables the communist functionaries to enforce the "One Child Policy."

The government, however, controls all media outlets in China exactly as I saw the Nazis do; only in this case it controls more than a billion people and there is a vast complex of media outlets. Former Chinese propagandist, Qinglian He, listed them recently at a hearing of the US-China Economic Security Review Commission July 31, 2007. According to the Web site of this commission and various media channels, Mrs. He, a Senior Research Scholar at Human Rights in China, included newspapers, periodicals, news agencies, TV stations, broadcastings, the movie industry, and art performers in her list of media outlets.

In order to better shape the thinking of the population, the education system is also controlled through government-published text books. This enables the regime to influence the emerging generations at a very early age. Similarly, the manipulation of the media is achieved through controlling its editors and journalists thus enabling the government to "mislead the Chinese population away from the values of Human Rights and Democracy and from truth as well," as stated Qinglian He. She also said that the United States is defined as the number one enemy of China.

The control system is executed by the Communist Party's Central Department of Propaganda and Government Disinformation. This brings us back to the Nazis. Joseph Goebbels was the minister for Propaganda and National Enlightenment. He had a major part in preserving a docile and obedient population that would support Hitler until the end of the war. The Nazi spin doctor achieved his objectives by deceiving the nation about the reality of the government's motives and historical developments. That is why he is called Hitler's chief liar.

All Americans are subject to mind control in various degrees. A Congress not committed to truth, the legal distortions from many courts, including the Supreme Court, and the lies of the government and main stream media, bind us to a godless and corrupt institution like the United Nations. They have created a cloud of lies that blankets our society like fog and obscures the truth. However, the internet, radio talk shows, books, quite a number of conservative and Christian Television networks and stations, and an army of people who fight against perversions forced upon us make mind control at least more difficult.

The so-called "fairness doctrine" promoted by the party of lies and abortion, which is touted as an instrument to create fairer reporting, has nothing to do with fairness. In reality it is an attempt to cripple or silence Christian and conservative radio talk shows which are a constant annoyance to the Socialists who are falsely called Liberals.

It should be a signal to all Americans about the direction some people like John Kerry have in mind for this nation. Edward Kennedy's "hate crime" project, has already penetrated the United States Senate, and has a transparent objective. The deceptive legislation has little to do with hatred but is instead crafted to protect homosexuals and repress the pro-life movement. It is part of a legal structure crafted for a perverse Socialist mind control system in the United States. If the promoters of this kind of legislation get their way we shall end up in a situation like the people of Shenzhen. They are the enemies within!

THE QURANIC CONCEPT OF WAR

The definition of terrorism as an instrument of warfare was produced by the Pakistani military. Brigadier General S. K. Malik defines in his book *The Quranic Concept of War* that the lesser the physical resources of a nation are, the greater the stress and reliance on the spiritual dimension of the war must be. The foreword to his book was written by General M. Zia-Ul-Haq, then Chief of Staff of the Army before he became president of Pakistan. He praises Malik and the book and writes, "This book brings out with simplicity, clarity and precision the Quranic philosophy on the application of military force, within the context of the totality that is JIHAD." The Cambridge Encyclopedia defines Jihad as "holy war." "According to the Koran, Muslims have a duty to oppose those who reject Islam, by armed struggle if necessary, and jihad has been invoked to justify both the expansion and defense of Islam."

Malik defines terrorism as a way for the weak to defeat the strong, because one can hit the enemy by making no distinction between civilian and soldier anywhere he so chooses. "The lesser the physical resources, the greater must be the stress and reliance on the spiritual dimension of the war." The unlimited resource of Muslims, who are willing to sacrifice their lives, is part of the spiritual dimension. But this 'spirituality' is based on an absurd lie promoted by Islamic religious leaders, that killing the enemy will lead to a reward in heaven for the killer in the form of 72 virgins put at his disposal. "To install terror into the hearts of the enemy is essential, in the ultimate analysis, to dislocate his faith. An invincible faith is immune to terror. A weak faith is the inroad to terror." I have not yet figured out what reward female terrorists are promised by the Muftis. Do they need to be lesbians in the in their concept of afterlife?

Islam cannot be taken seriously as a religion as long as this lie of rewarding killers of innocent women and children in Heaven is not rejected by all Islamic religious and political leaders, nor can it be taken seriously until the incitement of hatred in its school books, its media, and by governments is heralded as evil and abandoned. "The final stage of history will be the domination of all Christian countries by Islam and the extermination of all Jews," declared Sheikh Ibrahim Mudeiris, the religious leader of the Palestinian Authority, in a sermon on Friday May 13, 2005. "Israel has no right to exist." Since Abbas has not objected, this is also his purpose which is being financed by the West.

This is also the policy of the president of Iran, Mahmoud Ahmadinejad.

It is important to register what I describe in this chapter. Those who justify terrorism as a legitimate instrument of war are not just the clergy but the military as well. That puts the theory in doubt, which maintains that those engaged in terrorism are a small minority of radicals within Islam, a religion defined in the West as peaceful. I have read the Koran from beginning to the end and didn't find anything like "love your neighbor as you love yourself" or similar moral imperatives. It is more of a merciless warrior religion. Let me quote some of the suras:

The unbelievers among the people of the book (we Christians) and the pagans shall burn forever in the fire of Hell. (Sura 98:7)

Unbelievers are those who declare: Allah is the Messiah, the son of Mary. (Sura 5:17)

If you meet the unbelievers on the battlefield strike off their heads. (Sura 47:5)

…men have status above women. (Sura 2:228)

The unbelievers are your sworn enemies. (Sura 4:101)

The Messiah, Jesus, the son of Mary, was no more than Allah's apostle… (Sura 4:171)

The definition of a Muslim consists of five criteria: 1. One has to testify that there is only one God and that Mohammed is his prophet (shahada); 2. One has to pray five times a day at defined hours with the face toward Mekka (salt); 3. You have to give alms for purposes defined in the Koran (zakat); 4. Fast during the month of Ramadan, the ninth month of the Muslim calendar, (saum); 5. Make a pilgrimage at least once a lifetime to Mekka (haji).

With other words, religious fulfillment is achieved by complying with exterior criteria and not with moral or spiritual truth. That is why there is room in Islam for brutal murdering. Allah is not identical with God and Mohammed is not a prophet of our God. I don't think that Mohammed rose to Heaven from Jerusalem. He might have fallen in the opposite direction from somewhere else. The mosques erected in Jerusalem are not for the glory of God but to this day an attempt to destroy Judeo/Christian holy places.

Followers of Islam, like any other religion including Christians of today, have to measure their teachings and the understanding of them by the absolute moral standards of the Ten Commandments and the Sermon on the Mount.

THE PLO, HAMAS, HEZBOLLAH AND OTHERS

Not understanding the ideological power, motivation, and purpose of our enemies led to the Gaza disaster. While with one hand the American leaders are trying to build a terrorist-free democratic society in Iraq, with the other they are creating a Hamas terrorist state at the doorstep of Israel. Iraqi Prime Minister Nouri al-Maliki showed a similar schizophrenia during his visit to Washington at the end of July 2006 when he defended Hezbollah, fighting at the same time at home, a life and death struggle against other terrorists who have the same disregard for human life. He has to consider Shiite formations in Iraq which sympathize with the Shiite Hezbollah and back his government. Bush leveraged the visit to his political advantage because he needs progress or the appearance of progress, so that the Republican Party does not lose the next elections.

Whatever Hamas leaders say in public, they are out to destroy the Jewish state and transform Gaza into an axis of global terrorism and world conquest for Islam. Hezbollah as an instrument of Iran has the same purpose and transformed Lebanon also into a center of global terrorism. They are committed to the destruction of Israel and Christianity and any cease-fire will be nothing but a tactical move. In an interview given to the French newspaper Le Monde, Internal Security Minister Avi Dichter, spoke against a possible Israeli withdrawal from Judea and Samaria. "If we stop arresting and imprisoning Hamas terrorists whilst the Palestinian Authority does not do anything, in short space of time Hamas will rebuild its infrastructures and seize power as it did in the Gaza Strip," he said. Dichter added, "Hamas is no longer a terrorist organization but a true army of terrorists of 15,000 men, organized like Hezbollah in Lebanon and also supported, like Hezbollah, by Iran" (Guysen Internarional News).

Mahmoud Abbas, president of the Palestinian Authority, whose other name is Abu Mazen, was the finance chief and right hand man of Yasser Arafat. Most likely he organized the financing of the terrorists who murdered Israeli athletes during the Olympic Games in Munich. He is a terrorist himself who plays the moderate democrat just like his masters in Moscow where he was awarded his doctorate based on the thesis that the Holocaust never took place.

To think, as Western politicians do, that a democracy and peace could grow out of a treaty with these kind of people is laughable. They are fooling themselves because if they don't, they wouldn't know what to do. Again, Heaven help us with such a leadership.

The menace of Islamic terrorism is visible to everybody, but it is only a distraction. It is Marxism/Leninism with a religious label based on the same hatred and morality that was the bedrock of Nazi ideology. Terrorism today, or at least a considerable part of it, is most likely guided by Soviet intelligence professionals like Jevgeniy Primakov, ex-spy chief of the Soviet Politburo and Middle East expert. Later he turned up as Russian prime minister.

In my judgment, even though the purpose of the terrorists is Islamic world power, they are an instrument of the KGB, which now rules Russia, in a similar way that Hitler was an instrument of Stalin.

Once America is down, the Soviets and Chinese would destroy Bin Laden and his crowd—if he is still alive—as well as the oil sheiks. Neither Israeli Prime Minister Olmert nor President Bush and his advisors understand that Hamas, Hezbollah, or any of the other Islamic terrorist organizations are not in the game because of some pieces of land and a Palestine state as the final goal.

That is only a tactical short-term goal. Like the Nazi leaders, they are not interested in the well-being of their people but instead use them for their ultimate power purposes. The destruction of Israel and the United States, and the establishment of a global Islamic Taliban theocracy is their ultimate purpose. And for every lie they produce to fool those they want to destroy they have received generous financial aid from their targeted victims.

It was not the Soviets, however, who established the foundations of terrorism in the Middle East of today. The Nazis did. Before World War II, Jews and Arabs had a harmonious relationship. Emir Faisal, head of the delegation representing 22 Arab states after WWI in 1919 to the Versailles Peace Conference formally recognized a British mandate for a Jewish Palestine and signed in the name of the Arab world the Faisal-Weizmann Agreement (see Annex). The British government had recognized a Jewish national home in Palestine previously, in 1917 in the Balfour Declaration. Chuck Morris states in his well documented book *The Nazi Connection to Islamic Terrorism* that "the Emir Faisal bin Hussein signed the formal agreement with his diplomatic counterpart Dr. Chaim Weizmann, who was at that time acting as head of the World Zionist Organization and who was also acting in his capacity as the accredited head of the Zionist delegation to the Paris Peace Conference. Additionally, in subsequent correspondence with Harvard Law School Professor and later Supreme Court Justice Felix Frankfurter, Faisal accurately referred to Jewish claims in Palestine as 'modest and proper' and offered the Jewish people "a hearty welcome home."

In another letter to him Faisal wrote, "We feel that the Arabs and Jews are cousins in race, having suffered similar oppression at the hands of powers stronger than themselves, and by a happy coincidence have been able to take the first step toward the attainment of their national ideals together." Morse points out that these views were shared by enlightened Arab leaders of that time who felt that the emerging Arab nations could benefit from the know-how of Jewish settlers coming into the area.

Emir Faisal bin Hussein was recognized as head of the entire emerging Arab world at the end of World War I. He was the son of Hussein bin Ali, Sherif of Mecca and later King of Hijaz. The family members are Hashemites and were accepted by the Arabs as direct descendants of the Prophet Mohammed. Faisal later became King of Syria and then King of Iraq. His brother Abdullah would become King of Palestine east of the Jordan.

Unfortunately the Nazis, through the Grand Mufti of Jerusalem, Haj Amin al-Husseini, introduced hatred of Jews into the area, blaming them for anything wrong under the sun. He started the denial of the right to existence of Israel and the Jews. In 1920 he helped organize the first large scale pogrom in 100 years in Palestine, and from there on, violence and hatred against the Jews escalated drawing in all other Arab states and later also non-Arab Muslim states like Iran. He was also involved in the bloody 1937–1939 riots in Palestine.

Arab opponents to this development were brutally purged and assassinated and Al-Husseini was largely responsible for the spread of socialist totalitarian concepts in Iraq. He was also responsible for the persecution of Jews that culminated in 1951–52 in the expulsion of 250,000 Jews from that country with little more than the shirts they were wearing. It set the stage for the subsequent power grab by Saddam Hussein and his Socialist Baath Party. The ruthless dictator was himself a disciple of the Grand Mufti.

In 1941, Al-Husseini arrived in Berlin, which became his residence until the end of the war. He was treated like a head of state and given a luxurious residence and a monthly payment of $10,000, most likely taken from funds stolen from the Jews. He was received by Hitler on November 18, 1941, in the presence of Foreign Minister Joachim von

Ribbentrop and met many of the Nazi leaders including Heinrich Himmler, the top leader of the SS. Hitler assured him that he would furnish positive and practical aid to the Arabs involved in the same uncompromising war against the Jews. Germany would destroy the Jewish element residing in the Arab sphere. The two men agreed to secretly fuel pro-Nazi Arab revolts.

Al-Husseini got involved with the Holocaust by helping to round up Jews for deportation in Hungary, Poland, Romania, and Yugoslavia. Himmler gave him regular tours through the Auschwitz Concentration Camp to show him how efficiently the death machinery was operating. The deputy of Adolf Eichmann, Dietrich Wisliceny, declared during the Nurnberg War Crimes Trials, "The Mufty was one of the initiators of the systematic extermination of European Jewry and had been a collaborator and advisor of Eichmann and Himmler."

From Berlin he organized conferences, uprisings, espionage, sabotage in the Middle East in favor of Nazi Germany, and talked over the radio to the Arab world calling for Arabs to fight America, Britain and the Jews. "If America and England will win the war, Jews will dominate the world," he stated, and talked about the establishment of a Nazi-Muslim dominion. He recruited the notorious Hanzar brigades in Bosnia, Albania, and Yugoslavia to take part in the war on the German side and act as a vanguard for a Nazi Muslim Army. Nazi Parties were established in Syria and other Arab states. Right after the war he helped thousands of German Nazis escape from Germany and set them up in the Middle East through operation Odessa. They were soon employed by Arab military, intelligence and propaganda services. For them the war was not over.

Al-Husseini replaced the traditional informal system of government with one modeled after the German central command system. Power centered around him causing his influence to grow in the surrounding Arab states. In Egypt he helped create a Young Egypt youth organization which adopted the Nazi slogan, "One Folk, One Party, One Leader," while his own Palestinian Arab youth group was called the Nazi Scouts. A popular Arab song of that day was "No more Monsieur, no more Mister, in Heaven Allah, on Earth Hitler."

The Palestine Liberation Organization (PLO) had Nazi style organizations and did not hide its adoration of Hitler. Yasser Arafat was another protégé of the Gran Mufti, and his soldiers used the Nazi salute. The commander of Arafat's elite military formation "Tanzim 17," Fawsi Salim el Mahdi, had the nickname "Abu Hitler." He had given his two sons the names Eichmann and Hitler. Al-Husseini had already met Adolf Eichmann in the thirties in Palestine.

He died in 1974. His successor that kept the flame of hatred burning was his disciple Yasser Arafat, the father of terrorism. It is not only sad that the Arab leadership is basing its policies on fraudulent assumptions fabricated by Nazi mentality, but that Western governments have also bought into the fraud and are basically advancing Nazi concepts without realizing what they are doing.

Western Christians with the exception of millions of American Christians don't understand that what matters is purpose linked to destiny and history, and not whether the Israelis make mistakes or accidentally killed some innocent people. Hamas, the Palestinian Authority, Hezbollah, Islamic Jihad, and other similar terrorist groups with the help of Islamic governments and the Soviets are out to destroy Israel as a stepping-stone to destroying the United States. The state of Israel is defending its very existence with its back to the wall. In spite of it, nearly a million Arabs were given Israeli citizenship with the same rights as Jewish citizens while the Arabs throw the Jews out. Doesn't that say something about the nature of the opposing parties?

In the context of this book I cannot go into the details of the story and have only given highlights to make the substance visible. Chuck Morse has researched and articulated the course of events in a masterful way and I can only recommend my readers take the time to read his book. Plenty of information is also available in the Internet.

When the Israeli armed forces responded to the kidnapping and murder of Israeli soldiers within Israel by Hezbollah and to their targeting Israeli civilian areas for their missile attacks in July 2006, their ground forces encountered a highly disciplined and well led terrorist fighting force. Additionally, they had become part of the political establishment, and had social services for the population. Faithful to the Chinese prescription they operated a decisive part of their military activity from within civilian resident areas. They used women and children as human shields for their own protection. According to Jan England, the UN Under-Secretary General for Humanitarian Affairs, "the Hezbollah is involving the Lebanese people by its cowardice and that is the reason why it is responsible for hundreds of civilian deaths."

This is exactly what happened to an observer post of the United Nations where four of their soldiers were killed by Israeli bombs. Kofi Annan, the then anti-Israel UN secretary general, accused the Israeli armed forces of a deliberate attack against the United Nations. The following however is what really happened according to Jed Babbin, former U.S. deputy undersecretary of defense, who wrote in an Opinion Journal column:

"The UN's years-long record on the Israel-Lebanon border makes a mockery of the term 'peacekeeping.' On page 155 of my book "Inside the Asylum" is a picture of a UN outpost on that border. The UN flag and the Hezbollah flag fly side by side. Observers told me the UN and Hezbollah personnel share water and telephones, and that the UN presence serves as a shield against Israeli air-strikes against the terrorists."

Canadian Major General Lewis Mackenzie said during an interview on CBC radio that the Canadian peacekeeper killed during the above mentioned air strike had previously emailed him telling him that Hezbollah was using their post as cover and that he was taking fire very close, in one case three meters, but that the Israelis were targeting Hezbollah and not UN personnel.

Incompetent Marxist Kofi Annan demanded an apology from Israel, which he got. But an apology should have come from him. What was the UN doing there in the first place and who was paying for it?

The refugee camps around Israel have been used for the training of terrorists while the oil-rich Arab states did nothing to help those people. Neither did the UN "observers" do anything about it. We shouldn't pay for Annan's charade.

SOVIET INVOLVEMENT

In his article "Israel Humbled by Arms of Iran" in the *Telegraph*.co.uk, Adrian Blomfield writes that Israeli troops in the Lebanon war had found Soviet arms like the AT-5 Spandrel antitank missiles as well as eight Kornet anti-tank rockets, which Hizbollah terrorists left behind. On the boxes it said "Customer: Ministry of Defense of Syria. Supplier KBP, Tula, Russia."

I put this fact at the beginning of this chapter in order to make the players in our war against terrorism visible as we have to deal with each one of them if we are serious. It is not enough just to fight the executioner of a proxy war. The preparation of this war took decades. It was the KGB which told Yasser Arafat to declare war against America.

Yasser Arafat was always in the center of Soviet attention about whom I wrote earlier in this book. In the intelligence net of the Eastern European services subject to Soviet orders, Rumania was in charge of Syria, Lebanon and Lybia. Pacepa had to say the following, which was published in the *Jewish Virtual Library* on the basis of information from the *Wall Street Journal* September 24, 2003:

> Before I defected to America from Rumania, leaving my post as chief of Rumanian intelligence, I was responsible for giving Arafat about $200,000 in laundered cash every month throughout the 1970s. I also sent two cargo planes to Beirut a week, stuffed with weapons and other supplies to Beirut. Other Soviet bloc countries did the same.
>
> I was given the KGB's "personal file" on Arafat. He was an Egyptian bourgeois turned into a devoted Marxist by KGB

intelligence. The KGB had trained him at its Balashikha special-ops school east of Moscow and in the mid 1960 to groom him as the future PLO leader. First, the KGB destroyed the official records of Arafat's birth in Cairo, replacing them with fictitious documents saying that he had been born in Jerusalem and was therefore a Palestinian by birth.

The KGB disinformation department then went to work on Arafat's four-page tract called "Falastinna" (Our Palestine), turning it into a 48-page monthly magazine for the Palestinian terrorist organization al-Fatah. Arafat had headed al-Fatha since 1957. The KGB distributed it throughout the Arab world and in West Germany, which in those days played host to many Palestinian students.

"The terrorist war, per se, came into action at the end of 1968, when the KGB transformed airplane hijacking, that weapon of choice for September 11, 2001, into an instrument of terror," writes Pacepa in his article "Russian Footprints" in the *NationalReviewOnline*. He goes on to say,

In 1969 alone there were 82 hijackings of planes worldwide, carried out by the KGB-financed PLO. In 1971, when I was visiting Sakharovsky at his Lubyanka office, he called my attention to a sea of red flags pinned onto a world map hanging on the wall. Each flag represented a captured plane. "Airplane hijacking is my own invention," he said.

The political "success" occasioned by hijacking Israeli airplanes prompted the KGB's 13th Department, known in our intelligence jargon as the "Department for Wet Affairs" (wet being a euphemism for bloody), to expand into organizing "public executions" of Jews in airports, train stations, and other public places. In 1969, Dr. George Habash, a KGB puppet, explained: "killing one Jew far away from the field of battle is more effective than killing a hundred Jews on the field of battle, because it attracts more attention. By the end of the 1960's the KGB was deeply involved in mass terrorism against Jews, carried out by various Palestinian client organizations.

Yuri Andropov, KGB chairman and later the president of the Soviet Union, commented on these developments as a great opportunity to inject hatred with Marxist/Leninist thinking into the Muslim mentality of nationalism and victimhood, "and whip up the oppressed mobs to a fever pitch."

In the seventies Eastern bloc intelligent services sent hundreds of party activists into the different ethnic groups of the Islamic Middle Eastern countries as doctors, teachers, nurses etc. in order create hatred against American Zionism and train them in disinformation and terrorist operations. According to a rough estimate, which Pacepa received from Moscow, by 1978 the whole Soviet bloc intelligence community had sent some 4,000 such agents of influence into the Islamic world.

The same pattern of subversion is likely to gain strength in Latin America by the combined efforts of Cuba, Venezuela and Soviet Russia. There is detailed information on the KGB activities attempting to destroy us.

CHAPTER ELEVEN

THE STATE OF ISRAEL

ISRAEL BECAME A state in 1312 B.C., two millennia before Islam existed. Arab refugees from Israel began calling themselves "Palestinians" in 1967, two decades after the creation of the modern state of Israel. Upon conquering the land in 1272 B.C., Jews ruled it for one thousand years and maintained a continuous presence there for 3,300 years. The only Arab rule following conquest in 633 B.C. lasted 22 years. For over 3,300 years Jerusalem was the Jewish capital and was never the capital of any Arab or Muslim entity. Even under the rule of Jordan, the existing Palestinian Arab state created by Britain, (East) Jerusalem was not made the capital and no Arab leader came to visit it. Jerusalem is mentioned 700 times in the Bible, but not once is it mentioned in the Quran. King David founded Jerusalem; Mohammed never set foot into it. In 1948, Arab leaders urged their people to leave, promising to cleanse the land of Jewish presence. Sixty-eight percent of them fled without ever setting eyes on an Israeli soldier.

Virtually the entire Jewish population in Muslim countries had to flee as the result of violence and Pogroms. They were robbed of all their belongings and probably billions of dollars. These are the facts:

Jews in Arab Countries

	1948	2007
Algeria	140,000	0
Egypt	75,000	100
Iraq	135,000	100
Lebanon	5,000	100
Lybia	38,000	0
Morocco	265,000	5,700
Syria	30,000	100
Tunisia	105,000	1,500
Yemen	55,000	200

There are 840,000 Jewish refugees. According to the Unity Coalition for Israel they had to leave their assets behind currently worth more than $300 billion. Heskel M. Haddad, president of the World Organization of Jews from Arab countries, said that his organization has legal property deeds from Jewish refugees of a total area of 100,000 square kilometers, 3.5 times larger than the State of Israel. Irvin Cotler, an international human rights lawyer, Canadian parliamentarian, and former Canadian justice minister stated that UN documents reveal "a pattern of state-sanctioned oppression of refugees of Arab countries—including Nurnberg-like laws." Was that discussed in Annapolis?

Seven hundred and twenty-five thousand Palestinian Arabs living within the borders of Israel fled or were expelled in 1948. Today nearly one million Arabs live as citizens within the borders of the state Israel. It is rather strange to hear that today there are 4 million Arab refugees. Where do they come from? And why didn't affluent Arab leaders drenched in oil money look after their own Arab people for 60 years? Because they have a Nazi-like lack of concern for their fellow men and enslave their women. They use those who live in the camps to pressure Israel—this is the dirty purpose of those camps.

In the year 2007, Islam and Judaism's Holiest Holidays overlapped for 10 days. During this brief time Muslims racked up 397 dead bodies through 94 terrorist attacks in 10 countries. While they were busy spilling innocent blood, Jews on the other hand, celebrated their 159th Nobel Prize Winner.

There have been five wars against Israel by Arab nations all started by the Arabs. During the Jordanian occupation, countless Jewish holy sites were vandalized. The UN was silent when the Jordanians destroyed 58 Synagogues in the old city of Jerusalem. It continued its silence while Jordan systematically desecrated the ancient Jewish cemetery on the Mount of Olives, and remained silent when Jordan enforced Apartheid laws preventing Jews from accessing the Temple Mount and the Western Wall. Out of 175 United Nations Security Council resolutions up to 1990, 97 were against Israel, out of 690 General Assembly Resolutions, 429 were against Israel.

"It is a history mandated commitment of German policy to stand up for the right to existence of Israel," stated chancellor Merkel on July 28, 2006. Becoming an American citizen doesn't change my own personal commitment to stand up for the rights of the Jewish people which I promised God in 1950 as part of my restitution for the Nazi crimes committed in the name of Germany.

Olmert as well as President Peres, misjudging the motives of their enemies, seem to think that delivering more and more Israeli land to the Arabs will lead to peace. All the land for peace initiative will lead to is putting the Jewish state in extreme danger. I interviewed Shimon Peres some years ago in Tel Aviv at which time he told me that the need of the hour is to open the Israeli frontiers. I thought that he was very naïve in pushing Israel into sacrificing more of their land for the wrong reasons.

The United States is preparing another disaster which will come to light only when the Bush administration leaves the White House. The conference in Annapolis in November 2007 was a waste of money. No wonder that Arab leaders urge a strong U.S. role in Israel/Palestinian peace talks. Hearing President Bush talk about "occupied territories" it is easy to see that he has accepted their diabolical reasoning.

I thought Bush was a Christian, president or not. Who is he to undo God's promises to the people of Israel? I've also heard him say that democracy leads to peace, yet I cannot help but wonder what democracy he is referring to. I find it hard to believe he means American democracy, because less than 50 percent of the eligible voting body turns up on Election Day.

Countless insults are repeatedly exchanged by politicians in Washington, flying in the face of peace, which must begin in the hearts of men out of which they speak and negotiate. Therefore I am inclined to think that his assertion that democracy leads to peace is not true. Actually, democracy is not mentioned in our Constitution and we are in fact, a Republic.

Prime Minister Olmert stated that he speaks for his nation. Is that really so? A survey conducted by the "Midgam" Institutes reveals that 73 percent of the Israeli population refuses any concession on Jerusalem that is not approved by a referendum. In addition, 70 percent of respondents believe that Jerusalem cannot be the capital of both countries at once, according to Guysen International News. Another poll undertaken shortly before Olmert's departure to Annapolis sponsored by the Israel Policy Center for Promoting Parliamentary Democracy and Jewish values in Israeli Public life oppose handing strategic territory to the Arab Palestinians.

Our founding fathers were crystal clear that a free society can only exist with responsible and moral people. That is true for any society. Here we deal with liars and terrorists. According to Guysen International News the Mufti of Jerusalem, Ikrema Sabri, stated recently during an interview by the Jerusalem Post, "There has never been a temple on the Mosque Esplanada." He thinks that instead we should not talk about the "Temple Mount" but about the "Al Aqsa" mosque. I am pretty sure that most if not all Arabs at the Annapolis Conference not only believe the same and therefore are committed to a lie, but are determined to liquidate the basis of Western civilization in their midst, the thousands of years old Israeli heartland.

Western leaders including President Bush are denying our roots and capitulate to the aggressive Islamic lies.

I don't like the creation of 12 departments by the White House to monitor the "peace" process. These bureaucrats are not neutral if they start with the concept of "occupied territories." America should back up Israel but let them develop their own strategy to defend themselves. The road taken now will never lead to peace since hatred rules the hearts of the so-called partners for peace.

And what about the brilliant Israeli proposition of Benno Elon, which I wholeheartedly support?

He describes the Israeli borders set by God when He gave it as a gift to Abraham and his descendants in his booklet *Israel, Arabs & The Middle East*. Nowhere in the Bible is there any indication that God cancelled His promises. Cohen explains:

"The God-given borders of the land belonging to Abraham's descendents through Isaac are from 'the River' of Egypt (the Nile, or a smaller wadi in the Eastern Sinai) to 'The River' (the biblical name for the Euphrates…). These two border descriptions have never been fully occupied by the Jewish nation, but they stretch from Eastern Egypt past Damascus all the way into modern Western Iraq."

Hamas leader Haniyeh said at an election victory news conference that Hamas will "complete the liberation of other parts of Palestine." The Hamas Charter states in article 13, "Peace initiatives, the so-called peaceful solutions and international conferences are all repugnant to the beliefs of Hamas." On the Hamas Web site you could read what these godless Neo-Nazis think: "My message to the loathed Jews is that there is no god but Allah, we will chase you everywhere. We are a nation that drinks blood and we know that there is no blood better than the blood of Jews. We will not leave you alone until we have quenched our thirst with your blood, and our children's thirst with your blood."

Sheik Abdul Hadi Palazzi, Secretary General of the Italian Moslem Association vigorously refutes the Muslim extremist position which is that Islam is at war with Judaism, explains Chuck Morse. "This was the position embraced by al-Husseini and remains a mainstay of the Moslem Brotherhood, the Wahabi, Hamas and extremist Islamic group in general." Sheik Palazzi put it this way: "The idea that Islam should prevent Arabs from recognizing any sovereign rights of Jews over Palestine is quite recent and can by no means be found in Islamic classical sources…All parties must understand that Jews should never agree to have fewer rights than other religions, and Israelis will never agree to see David's capital divided in two parts."

In the ideological warfare in the Middle East the truth reaches the surface that the three godless ideologies of hatred, the Nazi ideology, the Marxist/Communist Soviet ideology, and the Islamic terrorist ideology, are cousins, branches that grow from the same root—the lie—and share the same purpose—world conquest. Sixty years after the end of World War II, the United States is at war with the ideology of the militarily defeated and eliminated National Socialist state. At the same time the country is at war with the class-war Communist ideology, an ideology that is supposed to have been defeated in the Cold War without recognizing the fact.

More than once I have heard President Bush say, that we have to deal with the "root causes" of what is happening in the Middle East. He is right but he doesn't go far enough. He means, I suppose, that terrorism must be eliminated. I agree with him on this. There is no way one can negotiate with terrorists. What is driving them is purpose rooted in hatred and it must be addressed and answered. The enemy has to be defined and be dealt with as a whole, with his worldview, his ideology, and his action.

Following that logic however means that in addition to the terrorist organizations, Iran and Syria have also declared war on the United States and Israel. The head of counter-terrorism at the state department confirmed that Iran "has complete command and control of Hezbollah."

The most important question in handling that situation is, whether it will be possible for the opposition within Iran to overthrow the government. The son of the last Shah has to be helped as much as possible.

The role of Soviet Russia under KGB agent Vladimir Putin has to be kept in the open all the time. They provide technology and weapons to Iran and train their people, leaving no doubt that as I said before, Putin is not our friend, he is our enemy.

Since Israel ceded the Gaza Strip to Arab Palestinians this area is slowly developing into a terrorist haven preparing itself for war against the Jewish state. Weapons enter the "country" via tunnels from Egypt. Never learning from history, even as history unfolds today, the Olmert administration is now negotiating and preparing to cede a great part of the West Bank if not all. The Israeli government is also being put on notice by the Arabs that peace could only be achieved by adding the Temple Mount and Eastern Jerusalem to the ceded package. Additionally Arab Refugees must be allowed to return to Israel. They would overrun the Jews because of their numbers.

Eighty percent of the Israeli settlers who were forced out of their homes in the Gaza Strip in 2005 by their own government are now in 2008 living in trailers, without land and a future in spite of the promises they received from Olmert and his staff. It seems that similar procedures are being prepared by the Israeli police for the West Bank.

The Syrian government declares that they are not interested in war against Israel but that the minimum condition for a peace treaty is the return of the Golan Heights to Syria. At the same time, hundreds of missiles of this Arab state are poised for a possible first strike against Israel, according to a report by the World Tribune.com of July 27, 2007. Israeli military sources say that the Scuds C and D as well as the SS-21 missiles could reach virtually any part of the Jewish state. These missiles of course come from Iran. Iran in turn is armed by UN Security Council members Soviet Russia and Red China.

If war were to break out between Israel and Syria, the Israeli Defense Force would conquer Damascus in a few hours, according to a report by the CSIS, the American Center for Strategic and International Research as reported on August 13, 2007, by Guysen International News. The supremacy of the Israeli air force over that of the Arabs should suffice to neutralize the Syrian air force and DCA systems in a few hours.

Hezbollah is also preparing for war with weapons from Iran. The United Nations military contingent charged the task to keep the two sides apart seems to be of no relevance. Iran also sends trained Hezbollah terrorists to Iraq to train a new generation of terrorists.

Regarding Western policies, insanity seems to reign. As usual our political leaders can only think in terms of election cycles and money, sending the latter to incompetent Arabs without giving them clear conditions for it. It boils down to the fact that the West is bankrolling the blackmailing of Israel by its enemies. Abbas even sends the European Union a request for billions of dollars in order to be able to pay salaries.

There should be no money from Western nations invested in the Gaza Strip or the West Bank as long as teachers and politicians, schoolbooks, and the media promote hatred against Israel and the United States. As long as rockets are fired at Israeli civilians, Arab terrorists prepare for war against Israel, and kidnapped Israeli soldiers are not returned.

Arms delivered to the Palestinian Authority find their way into terrorist hands which is why the partner for peace must be in full control of this area. I am afraid that the necessary controls will never be put in place. But it does beg the question, why should they come to the West for money and not, for instance, to Saudi Arabia?

There is no parallel in history for refugee camps lasting for 60 years. The Arabs could have learned how to integrate Arab refugees from Germany after WWII.

It is also clear that there will be no peace on the basis of the Bush/ Abbas/Olmert "peace plan" as long as the clerical terrorist government establishment in Iran remains in place. Instead of forcing their deficient concepts on Israel, Western leaders should give the tiny nation a free hand to defend itself.

Finally, there is an Israeli peace plan on the table put forward Benny Elon, who is chairman of the National Union Party and a member of the Knesset Foreign Affairs and Defense Committee. "The actions of the Israeli governments to establish a Palestinian state have not brought about peace but rather a whirlpool of blood," said Elon according to an article of Aaron Klein published by *WorldNetDaily* on November 23, 2007.

Elon refers to the billions of dollars wasted on the Israeli-Arab conflict. His plan suggests, that the Arabs living in the 59 UN maintained refugee camps be given rehabilitation packages and the option of moving to outside participating countries, where agencies would work to help with resettlement, employment, and housing solutions. Arabs who wish to remain in the West Bank would become Jordanian citizen. The plan calls for the disintegration of the Palestinian Authority and Israel's continued control of the West Bank, which are the biblical territories of Judea and Samaria.

Elon's plan, called the Israeli Initiative, has already found support in the Knesset and the United States Congress. Former Prime Minister Benjamin Netanyahu, chairman of the Likud Party read from the plan at the Knesset plenum in a show of solidarity.

According to a 2004 poll, 50 percent of the Palestinian Arab "refugees" would not rule out the option of moving to another country, if they had the ability and means to relocate.

A Palestinian state is not viable. There is no government in control of the area which is proposed for the Palestinian Arab state, terrorist attacks on Israel continue, hatred is being taught in education and promoted by the "state" media, they not only have no national income but seem to be incapable of creating it and depend on hand-outs from the wrong nations, and on top of it there is a need for an outside military force to contain further violence. What kind of state is that? And why should we with our tax money sustain terrorists? We face the brilliance of our Western politicians!

CHAPTER TWELVE

THE ENCIRCLEMENT OF AMERICA

WE ARE WITNESSING the formation of an anti-God and anti-American alliance, which aims at the destruction of free society and its standard bearer, the United States of America. Most disturbing is the lack of attention by the State Department and our intelligence services given to this gathering storm.

The Latin-American left leadership, the Chinese Communists, and the Arab terrorists and/or their sponsors are joining forces. At the beginning of May 2005, an Arabic-South-American summit took place in the Brazilian capital Brasilia. Arab Palestinian President Mahmoud Abbas was present. The summit was opened by the Communist Brazilian President Luiz Ignacio Lula da Silva, who attacked the "rich nations" and social inequalities. The main theme at the conference was to gain more economic independence from Europe and the United States. That of course is just the double-speak for the formation of an anti-American alliance, which is based on hatred. The participating representatives of different nations decided to intensify economic, cultural, and technological exchanges and coordinate their positions in international economic and commerce issues. The "right of states and people to resist foreign occupation" was part of the platform decided upon.

With other words, Abbas received an endorsement for past and future terrorism.

The Chinese President, Hu Jintao, visited Brazil in November of 2004, where he began his Latin American tour, to confirm China's commitment to a strategic relationship with Brazil. He promised investments of $5–7 billion predicting with President Lula, China would replace the United States as Brazil's top trading partner. Should that happen, Lula and other colleagues of his will show their true face. In the Argentine he promised investments of $20 billion and also confirmed China's commitment to their strategic partnership. Hu Jintao also visited Chile, where he established commercial links between the two countries, and Cuba, where I suppose he discussed with Castro how to take down the United States.

The Panama Canal is already in the hands of China. Now China is endeavoring to deprive the United States of their oil supply. On January 20, 2005, 13 agreements of the Statement on Energy Cooperation were signed in Beijing by Chinese Premier Wen Jiabo and Canadian Prime Minister Paul Martin, pledging cooperation in oil and gas, minerals and other sectors. I consider this an enormous scandal with U.S. foreign policy absent.

China's biggest state-owned oil companies, Petro-China and Sinopec, will contract to purchase oil from the Athabasca sands of Alberta. The oil is not in underground wellspring of liquid crude, but a vast expanse of oil-soaked sands and clays of several of that province's rivers. The reserves of crude oil from these sands are estimated to be 300 billion barrels. That tops Saudi Arabia's reserves.

The Chinese will acquire a controlling participation in a Calgary based Canadian energy company that is successfully developing a pair of oil sand sites. Also state-owned China Minmetals, Inc. has negotiated to buy Toronto-based resources and mining giant Noranda. More than 100 individual trading agreements have been inked between Chinese and Canadian companies—not only in oil but also in energy, resources, technology, and agriculture.

A 720 mile Canadian oil pipeline from northern Alberta west to the British Columbia coast is being planned which should have the capacity to transport 400,000 barrels of oil per day to serve China's demand for oil. The Canadian energy company has offered state-owned Chinese interests, a 49 percent ownership in this huge pipeline.

In May 2004, the Brazilian oil company Petrobras and China Petrochemical Corporation signed an agreement for a joint exploration of Brazilian offshore oil resources. The two companies agreed to cooperate on all aspects of petroleum production: extraction, refinement, sales and transportation.

Venezuela, the fifth largest oil exporter in the world, sells half of his oil production to the United States, but Chavez made it clear, that he wants to divert part, if not all of it, to China. Additionally the two nations signed 19 agreements, allowing Chinese companies greater access to 15 Venezuelan oil fields. The plans include Chinese investments in both oil and gas mining projects. China has signed 48 oil and resource investment and cooperation contracts with 20 supplier nations. Does the fact that Cuban teachers and intelligence officers are already there mean anything to our leadership?

We also need to remember that our Arab energy providers are dubious friends.

In Brazil, Cuba, and Venezuela there are hardcore Communists as heads of state. To the left are the presidents of Argentine, Nestor Kirchner and now his wife, who only recently re-established diplomatic relations with Cuba, Tabere Varquez in Uruguay, the first Socialist president in the history of this country, formerly Ricardo Lagos in Chile, who belonged to the Allende crowd and who was host to East German Communist leader, Honecker, when he went into exile, and now Michelle Bachelet, a Communist who lived in Communist East Germany for several years, Daniel Ortega in Nicaragua. Finally there are Alan Garcia in Peru, and Evo Morales in Bolivia. The socialist government establishments in Chile and in the Argentine are busy destroying their conservative armed forces by subverting and changing the law in order to eliminate those who could threaten their hold on power. The United States has no policy in place.

Then there is Columbia with a civil war which no government seems to be able to win. The FARC has become a multinational crime syndicate according to Jorge Noguera, head of Columbia's secret police, carrying out extortion rackets, training others in kidnapping, and providing drugs. Unstable conditions, which can deteriorate any time, exist in Ecuador and Haiti, Belize is full of Chinese.

The communist parties of nearly all Latin-America countries are members of the Sao Paulo Forum, which was created in 1990 under the official sponsorship of Fidel Castro and Lula da Silva, then president of Brazil's Communist Workers Party. It is a continuation of the Havanna Tricontinental Conference, set in motion by the Politburo of the Soviet Union in 1964.

In May of 2005 my friend Paul Trog wrote from Brazil, "On our recent trip to the South of Brazil (Feb./March of that year), I started to worry after reading in "Zero Hora," one of the leading papers of Porto Alegre, that the ABIM, Brazil's CIA, was planning to send some of their agents for training to Cuba. Havana's Secret Services has in its employment several Russian former KGB trainers that were to participate in the program. The same information was published in the 'Corrio do Povo,' also of Porto Alegre, and in the 'Folha de Sao Paulo.'"

Trog continued,

My worries were considerably enhanced after "Veja," the Time Magazine of Brazil, prominently published in its editions of March 16th 2005 and March 23rd 05 that the FARC of Colombia (a narco-terrorist army that threatens the democratically elected government of that country), had funneled millions of Dollars to Lulas' Partido Trabalista (PT) during the last elections (2002) which Lula won. In secret meetings at a ranch near Brasilia, the unofficial ambassador of FARC to Brazil, Father Medina, a catholic priest, had offered the money and outlined the transaction methods in detail. This information was submitted to the ABIM, the Brazilian intelligence service, by one of its agents who were present at the meetings. At that point, however, that information was buried in a top secret file and was successfully suppressed. Nevertheless, early this year, there was a "vasamento" (leak) and the ABIM had to confirm the veracity of the report, to the discomfort of its head, General Felix.

I remember that in the Sixties, Khrushchev had secretly ordered the infiltration of all the existing criminal organizations of the world, in order to satiate the West and our soldiers then in Viet Nam, with narcotics—and thus undermine the bourgeois democracies.

We visited also some friends and relatives in Ijui, a little town of approx. 100,000 inhabitants located in the Serra of Rio Grande do Sul. Ijui has a University founded by the Capucin Brotherhood, which is far to the left by reputation. We were informed that a full dozen of Russian professors were employed by the university.

CHAPTER THIRTEEN

ROBERT MUGABE
THE DISGRACE OF ZIMBABWE

BRITISH PRIME MINISTER Tony Blair, host and chairman of the G-8 summit in Gleneagles, Scotland, from July 6–8, 2005, focused the agenda on easing poverty in Africa and tackling climate change. In their final declaration, the eight leaders, without considering their own indebtedness, committed their nations to double the financial aid to Africa until 2010 from the present $25 billion to $50 billion. Shortly before the summit, 18 nations had already received complete debt relief, which most likely means, the international tax payers relieved the related banks from the consequences of their irresponsible lending. Fourteen of the recipients were from Africa. Between 1960 and 2000 Africa received $500 billion worth of financial aid. Nevertheless the African economy contracted 0.6 percent between 1975 and 2000. The United States is supposed to contribute $4 billion of the additional $25 billion. Now comes presidential candidate Barak Obama presenting a plan to the American people to add $185 billion to it "to fight poverty."

At the time of the summit, President Robert Mugabe destroyed an estimated 25 percent of the Zimbabwe economy within a month, using bulldozers to level the homes of about 1.5 million of his own citizens in what he called an "urban renewal campaign." From the first day of his presidency in 1980 Marxist/Leninist Mugabe accumulated a criminal record. He eliminated his black opposition by murdering thousands of them, harassed the white farmers, began to have them chased from their properties by mobs, practically destroyed the national agriculture, and committed mass murder of whole villages, mass rape, and torture. He can vote in the United Nations.

Zimbabwe, formerly South-Rhodesia, was not a British colony but a flourishing nearly independent nation within the Commonwealth, with its own Constitution and elected Parliament producing a government of both races. South Rhodesia was called the bread basket of Africa because of its highly developed agriculture and management. Black and white citizens had a bright future. The nation wanted full independence; Britain, however, had other ideas.

During all the years of the independence battle, all British governments insisted on the inclusion of Mugabe. For administrative purposes they wanted to combine their colonies, North Rhodesia and Malawi (Nyasaland) with South Rhodesia, which had a substantially advanced government and economic structure and was opposed to a Marxist configuration. There were also internal election and international image concerns in London. But the main push came from the African Marxists leaders, Kenneth Kaunda, Josua Nyerere, Hastings Banda, Samora Machel, and others who didn't want white or black conservative leaders around. When 29 tribal chiefs, the true leaders of the black population arrived in London after having traveled to India, Pakistan, and Europe to make their independence case, and having been received by the pope in Rome, the British prime minister refused to receive them.

Britain appeased the left-wing much as Chamberlain had appeased Hitler. The government denied South Rhodesia full independence, and with the help of the American and South African governments, manipulated the existing coalition out of power to installed Mugabe.

With no concern for the Rhodesian people the British establishment bears full responsibility for the disaster of Zimbabwe. Involved in this process of betrayal over the years were the Home-, Heath-, Wilson-,

MacMillan- and Thatcher-governments. Mugabe became rich, ruined the country, and destroyed the lives of Zimbabwe's people. Instead of lifting Africa to their own high level of development through their own efforts, Zimbabwe became the miserable recipient of foreign aid with a population close to starvation. And while there have been different versions of this same sordid tale, this is the story of the continent of Africa.

Then, with no recognition of his predecessor's failures and waste of money, Tony Blair organizes "Help for Africa" to overcome poverty and hunger. The G-8 "leaders" opened another brainstorming session to support the same failed Western policy. They enrich corrupt government receivers, and the "Lords of Poverty" as author Graham Hancock calls the international establishment of development, aid bureaucrats in indebting their taxpayers even more. We could learn from the Chinese who have invested heavily in Africa but avoid government involvement. They have created a reputation of helping people get jobs by directly overseeing infrastructure projects, like roads.

The Mugabe principle was applied to countless of other situations but is not restricted to Africa. In Gleneagle, G-8 decided to provide $3 billion to help the Palestinian Arab terrorists to form their own state. They simply don't want to learn. This money is not only wasted but finances our, and Israel's, deadly enemies. Money does not heal hatred, which destroys democracy. Hamas and Hezbollah have neither laid down their weapons nor given up their intention to destroy Israel, they simply pretend to be democrats now.

A friend of mine who has spent 45 years working in intelligence in rather senior positions commented to me that most of these kinds of arrangements "fail to fix the inherent problem." Our culture trying to come up with quick solutions never allows us to focus long-range on a problem. There are always countless "hot issues" that have to receive immediate attention and priority, and they tie up our assets to a point that long-range objectives are the exception rather than the rule. If that doesn't change it will destroy America.

At this writing, Mugabe has begun to steal the last financial pearl Zimbabwe has, the Zimplats Corporation, which operates one of the largest platinum mines in the world.

At the same time, Ian Smith, the last prime minister of South Rhodesia died at the age of 88 years. It was Smith that had made South Rhodesia the breadbasket of Africa together with the Black tribal leaders and their people. The reports about his death which I read in *Die Welt* in Germany, the *London Times,* and my local newspaper the *Press-Register,* were full of disgusting lies similar to what is being written worldwide about the former Chilean President Augusto Pinochet who is portrayed as a bloodthirsty dictator. On the other side, Communist Nelson Mandela has been promoted to a modern saint of democracy. These kinds of distortions are called brainwashing.

CHAPTER FOURTEEN

THE ENEMY WITHIN

THE ITALIAN COMMUNIST Gramski and the German Marxists of the Frankfurt School, who operated in the thirties from New York, defined the class enemy anew to encompass all civil and cultural institutions of Western society. Their new designation was applied to such establishments as schools, universities, the family, churches, and others. Abandoning the Marxist/Leninist revolutionary concept of taking over government from outside, by force if necessary, they settled in favor of a new methodology, to take over government, political parties, the media, some foundations, and social and political institutions from within. They do so by penetrating the minds of people and disconnecting them from their history and traditions. It is supposed to culminate in the destruction of the existing social order and freedom, ushering in a socialist-totalitarian government system.

The ACLU is spearheading the implementation of this concept bringing Nazi concepts and policies into the heart of American society. They are the real Neo-Nazis in contemporary America and it is here where the connection between National and international Communist Socialism appears to surface. To me, it is incredible that the ACLU is able to fund itself with taxpayer's money. Are the members of Congress out of their minds? Can't they understand that if they allow the undermining of God and his moral absolutes in society, that they are creating self-centered, irresponsible men and women? Facing the threats from inside and outside and with the difference between civilians and soldiers evaporating, the United States must have responsible citizens. And if you add to these activities devastating natural disasters then one must conclude that God is imperative to our national security.

What I said about Neo-Nazi movements is meant to make the reader understand the acute moral and ideological similarities between their philosophies in spite of their different background and labels. They hold the extreme positions of relativism, where neither morality nor concern for human life exists and hatred is their common motivation. The massive geo-political upheavals that shake our globe are driven by raging and organized hatred festering in the hearts of men. That is at the heart of each crisis point in the world of today.

However, the contempt of human life is not confined to terrorists and their like, we have it at the heart of our society. Even though the deplorable moral state of America did not develop by itself, and has been pushed on us for a long time with the intention to destroy us, to destroy a free way of life. The responsibility for it lies with those who make an immoral law, those who vote those legislators into power, and those who make use of it. There is a moral connection between the ruthlessness of the outside Neo-Nazis, the indifference to human life plaguing vast parts of American and Western societies, and the bystanders who watch the destruction of the moral fiber of our nations. It is the hideous face of the same common evil with different appearances. We are the enemy within: the self-centered me, myself, and I, who do what offends God. I have explained in detail my moral responsibility for an immoral government. In the same way every American is responsible for the moral foundation of this nation.

The Nazis denied God and went to great lengths to exile Him from German society as I explained earlier. The ACLU does exactly the same with a democratic label, which distorts both the letter and spirit of our Constitution. The Nazis legally declared the Jews to be non-persons and then murdered them. The Supreme Court of the United States legally declared the unborn human being to be a non-person, and set the stage for their legalized mass murder and called it abortion. Isn't that the same procedure the Nazis used for dealing with unwanted people? With a 5-4 decision, the Supreme Court forced Nazi contempt of human life in the disguise of concern for women on a supposedly Christian nation.

The reasoning consists of two lies. The first denies that life begins at conception, and the second that the body of a woman belongs to her, so she alone has the right to decide what to do with it. St. Paul states clearly that the body of every last person in this world belongs to God, and that it is the temple of the Holy Spirit. America will not defeat terrorism unless we end the terrorism against unborn human life. Where are the Christians? And where are our elected leaders?

According to statistics of the Guttmacher Institute and estimates by the National Right to Life Committee, 47 million legal abortions were performed from 1973 to 2005. Polls about the position of Americans regarding this procedure of killing unborn human beings show that the population is close to equally divided on the issue.

A Guttmacher poll asserted that the reason for 86 percent of America's abortions was for convenience and only 1 percent occurred because of rape. Since about 85 percent of Americans believe in God, there must be at least 35 percent who say they believe in God and in the righteousness of abortion. The two positions, however, are mutually exclusive. Men and women who vote "pro-choice" candidates into public office make themselves accomplices to murder.

America is short of about 50 million citizens. "That is higher than the population of some countries..." stated Randall K. O'Bannon, Director of Education and Research for the National Right to Life Committee. "That would be comparable to wiping out a number of whole states...The world was appropriately horrified and shocked when we lost a couple of thousand people on September 11...what we are talking about here is that sort of loss multiplied...our society needs to put into context the enormous amount of loss that we have suffered—the enormous amount of intelligence, the enormous amount of creativity, the enormous amount of productivity." I add the enormous loss of moral fiber. It is also reasonable to say that the invasion of illegal aliens could not have happened on the scale it has if the murdered babies had been born.

A corrupt judiciary is at the heart of the devastating decline of the moral vigor in American society and the alarming disintegration of family values. As godless judges in Nazi Germany made the law subject to Nazi ideology, many American judges push God aside as the source for law and justice, and in violation of the Constitution apply Socialist concepts as basis for their rulings. The reasoning is different but the principles are the same.

In Nazi Germany, films presenting the Nazi's perverse concepts of right and wrong made people accept godless laws and actions. Many films in America today project a different environment which, however, has the same intention: to destroy Christian faith and teachings. The Da Vinci code, where reality is subtly intermingled with lies carefully interwoven into the plot is a true part of the anti-God Alliance.

In a questionnaire, the Palmdale School District in California asked children between 7 and 10 years of age sexual questions about the frequency of "thinking about having sex," "having sex feelings in my body," "touching my private parts too much," and similar provoking insinuations. Parents had not been consulted. Enraged, six of them sued the school district. A three-judge panel unanimously ruled for the 9th Circuit Court of Appeals that there is "no fundamental right of parents to be the exclusive provider of information regarding sexual matters to their children…" and that parents "have no due process or privacy right to override the determination of public schools as to the information to which their children will be exposed while enrolled as students."

"I think that is one of the most frightening examples of judicial tyranny that has come down" said Dr. James Dobson in his daily radio broadcast pointing out that parents are being robbed of their right to educate their children. In a television interview on Fox News, Dobson called for the impeachment of Judge Stephen Reinhardt who had written the ruling. He quoted Article III Section I of the Constitution which says that Congress has the right to create and to control the courts below the Supreme Court. "And they won't use it," he added.

Hitler had the same intentions as these three judges and considered the youth to be the property of the Nazi State. He wanted the parents out of the way but didn't get to it because the 12 years he was in power were too short. Modern Socialists are getting closer. Already in my earlier book "*Moral Meltdown*" I wrote about the efforts by German Socialists in education to destroy the family. Similarly, the book entitled *Religion for Young People aged between 16 and 18* says, "The (desired) changes must reach down to the smallest cell in society, the traditional family which must be transformed into a large family—broader sexual links...Ultimately there must no longer be any private ownership of washing machines, women and children." A course book for religious education of 10–15 years old has the title *How Can Children Defend Themselves Against Their Parents?* It shows specific ways to evade the rules of the parents.

US District Judge Lawrence Karlton ruled that the Pledge of Allegiance in public schools is unconstitutional. It is his ruling, however, which is unconstitutional. Why is he not impeached?

California Governor Arnold Schwarzenegger signed a bill into law which instructs public schools to allow boys to use girls restrooms and locker rooms, and vice versa, if they chose. Parents have no say. He also signed bill SB777, sponsored by lesbian State Senator Sheila James Kuehl, which bans textbooks, references, teaching aids, activities, events, discussions, posters, announcements, workbooks and anything else within the public school system, from anything that reflects or promotes bias against homosexuality, transgenders, bisexuals, or those perceived gender issues. According to Keren England, executive director of the Capitol Resource Institute, "SB 777 is designed to transform our public schools into training centers for sexual experimentation to become institutions that disregard all notions of the traditional family unit. This reverse discrimination is an outright attack on the religious and moral beliefs of California citizen."

In Massachusetts, U.S. District Judge Mark L. Wolf ordered the gay agenda taught to Christians who attend a public school in the state, reasoning that they need the teachings to be engaged and productive citizens.

In Illinois, at Deerfield High School officials have ordered the fourteen–year-old freshman class into a "gay" indoctrination seminar, after having them sign a confidentiality agreement promising not tell their parents.

In Virginia, in the Albemarle School District the teachers were ordered to invite students as young as kindergarten to a promotion of a summer camp that advocates "Atheists, Freethinkers, Humanists, Brights or whatever…" The teachers who did not follow this order think that they opened themselves for repercussions.

Judge George Greer, backed by the judicial system, got away with condemning Terri Schiavo on faulty evidence to a slow and torturous death. If anything follows Nazi prescription, then this is it. Following an order, which Hitler gave right after the beginning of the war, the Nazis murdered hundreds of thousand people "unfit to live and of no use to society." Bielefeld, the city where I learned the languages I mentioned earlier, continues to be home to the Bethel Institute that looked after retarded people. When the Nazis came to pick them up for liquidation, the head of the Institute, Pastor Friedrich von Bodelschwingh, put up such a furious battle that they abstained. His courage thwarted their intentions regarding his institute but the murderous concept of euthanasia was carried out and led to the Holocaust. Arrogant contempt of human life is the common trade mark. For me men like Reinhardt, Karlton, and Greer who today implement the same Nazi philosophy of contempt of God, family, and human life are the true Neo-Nazis, pushing America into the direction of self-destruction.

It is also interesting that the doctors in Nazi occupied Holland refused as a body to comply with the Nazi request to deliver all disabled people to them for liquidation. Today Holland, followed by Belgium, leads Europe in immorality. Euthanasia has been practiced there for years and the medical community is subject to almost no restrictions. Tens of thousands of people have been killed by use of prescription drugs, which they thought were sleeping pills but contained poison instead.

Episcopal bishop V. Gene Robinson in February 2005, entered an alcohol treatment center to treat his alcoholism. He should have simply made a decision to stop drinking but obviously is unable to control his lusts. He left his wife and children to have sex on a regular basis with another man, whom he calls a partner. This is contrary to any concept of what it means to be a Christian. Not only he, but all those who made him a bishop are volunteers for the anti-God alliance.

Richard D. Lamm, former governor of Colorado, described "a secret plan to destroy America." In a speech to a stunned audience in Washington at a conference about immigration reform in 2004, he described how the enemy within could destroy his own country. Actions of individual people and groups are not necessarily coordinated. For different but normally selfish reasons they together pull America toward destruction. This is what Lamm advocated:

1. Make America a bilingual-bicultural country.
2. Invent "multiculturalism" and encourage immigrants to maintain their own culture.
3. Make the United States a "Hispanic Quebec." Celebrate diversity rather than unity.
4. Make our fastest growing demographic group the least educated.
5. Get big foundations and big businesses to give these efforts lots of money.
6. Establish dual citizenship and promote divided loyalties. "Celebrate diversity."

7. Place these entire subjects off-limits, make it taboo to talk about them. Use words like "racist," "xenophobe." Make it impossible to enforce our immigration laws.
8. Censor Victor Davis Hanson's book *Mexifornia*—this book is dangerous. He exposes my plan.

The end result of the above programs would be the transformation of a nation of patriots with the mission of freedom into a geographic region inhabited by a cultural mix of people who are separated from God, history, and tradition, and mainly interested in getting richer, having more sex, and believing in a toothless "Christian" religion. Such people can easily be manipulated by power-hungry politicians. And that is exactly what a considerable number of them have in mind.

Americans have to understand that the decisive battle line for our future is not between political parties—the Republicans and the Democrats for instance, even though the Democrats as a party are far ahead on the down side. The true line is between relative and absolute moral standards—between the dictatorship of relativism and the absolute truth of God. It is the ideological battle line that is so difficult for Americans to understand. From top to bottom of any party, institution, religious denomination, or any part of the media you have people with both positions. It is there where the battle rages and there can be no morally neutral warriors. Anybody who considers him or herself to be neutral is automatically on the side of relativism, and by default an enemy of God. A myriad of our institutions are already subverted and anti-American.

The polarization of American politics is a somewhat recent phenomenon. In fact, you will find elections and decisions on moral and social issues are relative at all levels of society. And in most Western countries the dominant influences come from two presiding political parties which have excluded the others from being major players. Unfortunately, such exclusivity is not in the best interest of any nation.

These influences, however, are the tip of the iceberg and beneath them are ideologies driven by mutually exclusive worldviews.

For example, abortion has polarized this country spawning quite a number of parallel issues it is equally divided over. Abortion, however, is a moral issue about what is right and what is wrong, which will never be resolved on the level of our two main political parties. That is the reason, why the campaign for the 2008 elections started 18 months before they take place.

The Democratic Party, which I call the Abortion and Liars' Party, wants to win the White House, and influence in Congress to establish rules that keep them in power forever. Their efforts are not for us, the people they have sworn to serve, but for strengthening their power base. Ideologically they are Socialists with a philosophy that bears a very disturbing resemblance to Marxism.

The connection between the enemies within and the enemies outside is the rejection of God and His moral absolutes. It is exactly the same issue I had to face after the end of the war but with a different set of rules: my moral responsibility for the Nazi disaster and the defining and appeasement of evil. Today, in America, the enemies within help the enemies outside tear down the moral infrastructure of our nation.

For example, Vladimir Putin is on the same God-denying side as the adulterer, womanizer, and perjurer Bill Clinton who vetoed laws passed by Congress to end partial birth abortion twice. His wife Hillary, who wants to become president, is following the same godless path of her husband. Together with Senators Charles Schumer and Barbara Boxer and others they have introduced, H.R. 1964 and S.1173, a bill which would reverse the decision of Congress and the President and undo the ruling of the Supreme Court regarding partial birth abortion.

Presidential candidate Rudy Giuliani says that he is against abortion but donated money to Planned Parenthood. That donation, he stated, "squares with my support of the right of choice." He wants to be on both sides of the issue and doesn't seem to know that there is no right to murder. He is morally neutral and therefore does not understand substance of freedom and the global ideological battle. That makes him part of the godless.

Coffee giant Starbucks imprinted the following message of a client on their cups: "Why in moments of crisis do we ask God for strength and help? As cognitive beings, why would we ask something that may well be a figment of our imagination for guidance? Why not search inside for the power to overcome? After all, we are strong enough to cause most of the catastrophes we need to endure."

Former Virginia ACLU chapter president Charles Rust-Tierny was arrested for receiving and processing graphic child pornography. No wonder he wants God out of business and the truth of our Constitution eliminated.

I apply to them the same standard as I applied and apply to myself when I look at my immorality with God's eyes. I had not taken part in the crimes of the Nazis but was as morally godless as they were. I am addressing moral and not criminal issues here meaning that in the way I lived I was closer to the Nazis than to God.

Bill and Hillary Clinton, Obama, Schumer, Boxer, Guiliani, Schwarzenegger, Bishop Gene Robinson, Putin, Judge Reinhardt, the general manager of Starbucks and Rust-Tierny to name only a few are part of the global anti-God alliance. Their concepts are godless and therefore their influence can only weaken America.

These are symptoms of a gradual erosion of moral absolutes in our society and the spreading of a tyranny of relativism. Neither in government nor individually do a large section of people know the difference between right and wrong any more. It has become my party, my plan, my profit, my side, my victory, my institution, my congregation or simply me, myself, and I. This development is accelerated by the aggressive penetration of pornography via the internet into the homes of people. We live in a perverse society where it is illegal to name God, Jesus Christ, and their Commandments in schools while at the same time it is legal to send hard core porn via the internet into the homes of citizens. It hasn't yet dawned on Congress that this will destroy a free America if it is not changed. It is the selfishness of ordinary people that opens the gate to immoral tyranny, just as it happened in Germany.

Christians call selfishness sin, and sin cripples. Crippled people cannot create and maintain a free society. Jesus called the liars slaves of the devil. Slaves are unfit to govern a free society.

Islamic terrorism feeds on the immorality of the enemy and terrorists are being recruited in America. "Terror can be instilled only if the opponent's faith is destroyed," explains Pakistan's General Malik as the reason for the need of terrorism as military instrument of war. "An invincible faith is immune to terror. A weak faith offers inroads to terror." It is the responsibility of the government to create in our society the conditions to strengthen the Christian faith of the American nation instead of destroying it. It is the responsibility of the Christian pastors and their flock to hold government accountable to do so.

Ronald Reagan stated, "God...should never have been expelled from American schools. As we struggle to teach our children...we dare not forget that our civilization was built by men and women who place their faith in a loving God."

Engraved in the Thomas Jefferson Memorial in Washington, D.C. are his words, "God who gave us life and gave us liberty. Can the liberties of a nation be secure when we have removed a conviction that these liberties are the gift of God? Indeed I tremble for my country when I reflect that God is just, that his justice cannot sleep forever."

Spirit One Christian Center Pastor Mark Holick, reported *World-NetDaily* in June 2007, told the IRS that his church will not stop teaching and preaching God's work, "even if it relates to contemporary issues in the world." The IRS had objected to a sign that read: "Sibelius [some politician] accepted $300,000.00 from abortionist Tiller, price of 100 babies." Pastor Holick pointed out that it is only part of a responsibility on the part of a Christian church to comment on abortion, a red-hot topic in the church's home city of Wichita in Kansas. If all American pastors and Rabbis would begin getting on this road and into the action, America would be different over night.

John Witherspoon, signer of the Declaration of Independence who served in 120 Congressional Committees, was President of Princeton University, and the only clergyman to sign the Declaration stated: "Whoever is an avowed enemy of God, I scruple not to call him an enemy of this country. It is in the man of piety and inward principle that we may...find the uncorrupted patriot, the useful citizen, and the invincible soldier...God grant that in America true religion and civil liberty may be inseparable."

WE THE PEOPLE DON'T WANT

— Judges who DENY the priority of the rights of the parents to determine the education of our children and grandchildren, and would instead have the state take over like in Nazi Germany.
— A left wing trade union to indoctrinate our children in our schools with godless Darwinism like in Nazi Germany.
—A government which lies to us, for example by giving us fabricated statistics regarding inflation.
— Representatives in Washington who steal our payments into Social Security and use that money for their own re-election by bribing their voters with perks.
— A government establishment which teams up with big business, not elected groups, and leaves us to the mercy of illegal aliens instead of complying with their oath of office to protect us and our property.
— To give away our sovereignty through secret manipulations and hidden traps in treaties.
— Allow godless politicians and judges to destroy the traditional family.

— To have the God of our founding fathers be expelled from government and schools.

— To feed and pay our enemies such as the United Nations.

— To allow profit motivated international bankers to decide money, supply, and interest rates.

The mentality of selfishness has to be attacked and confronted with God's absolute moral standards of absolute honesty, absolute purity, absolute unselfishness and absolute love. This has to be done especially in our schools and universities. Darwinism has to be thrown where it belongs: in the trash! We need a Christian revolution to clean up the mess and make America one nation under God, a lighthouse for the world.

CHAPTER FIFTEEN

NO TO THE NORTH AMERICAN COMMUNITY COLLECTIVE

THERE IS NO question in my mind that a serious attempt to destroy the constitutional sovereignty of the United States is underway. One road is the attempt to form an economic block of the three North American nations, promoted by our own government establishment. This would be accompanied or followed by eliminating frontiers within the block and launching a new currency, the Amero. The millions of illegal aliens automatically and without Congress would become legal, at the expense of the American taxpayers, it seems to me. The net effect of this block-building would be the end of our freedom and independence apart from being unconstitutional. It follows the pattern of the formation of the European Union which started with a Common Market 50 years ago. Thirty years later the project went into high gear.

White House press secretary Tony Snow was asked by Les Kinsolving of WND at a press briefing on July 12, 2007: "Will the president categorically deny any interest in building a European Union-style super state in North America?" He answered, "Of course, no. We're not interested. There is not going to be an EU in the U.S." This statement, however, cannot be taken seriously looking at the facts. A new currency replacing the dollar with the Amero will be the same currency used by Canadian and Mexican nations. This is identical with losing your independence. In other words, if it walks like a duck and talks like a duck, it is a duck!

It took Europe about fifty years to get to the Euro. Those who pull the strings in these global developments, whoever they are, now think that the ground is prepared for getting to the Amero in only six years. The suggestions how to go about it in a May 2005 report by an Independent Taskforce on behalf of The Council on Foreign Relations entitled "Building a North American Community," are not very different from what is already established in Europe. The president needs to publicly reject the Amero and its integration. Unfortunately I have not heard President Bush utter these words, because he is spearheading the project.

The international Soviet conspiracy teams up with big business and international bankers. It is not an alliance but each group follows its own purposes which in the short term happens to be the same. And then there are the globalists of the Council on Foreign Relations which think that national sovereignty is out of date. The complete abandonment of our borders, the secret preparations for the North American Union with Canada and Mexico, the insane protection program of the illegal aliens within the United States, the intimidation of the border agents by sending law abiding agents into prison and the effort to mold immigration legislation to the benefit of millions of illegal aliens from another culture against the will of the majority of the American people, but with their money, are ingredients of a program which will destroy this nation if it is allowed to be executed.

Special agent of the Immigration and Customs Enforcement Brian Moskowitz stated according to a report of *Reuters* of August 29, 2007, that in a raid of a chicken plant in Ohio in August 2007 160 illegal aliens were arrested. Among the charges these people face are illegal reentry to the United States, identity theft, document fraud, social security fraud, and forgery. This is most likely representative for a myriad of aliens. I find the years-long policy of our government to do nothing about it nearly unbelievable. It is as Congressman Tom Tancredo stated in a debate of Republican candidates for the presidency, the issue is not immigration but our state of law. Is our government anti-American?

The European Union exists already and I have described how it was created. According to a report "Now Africa Heads Toward Continental Government" by Jerome R. Corsi published in *WorldNetDaily* of August 6, 2007, the unification process is well-advanced. "On July 11, 2000, at the Lome Summit in Togo, the states constituting the Organization of African Unity, signed a declaration to form the 53-nation African Unity. Now they have already created executive, legislative, and judicial bodies required for regional government, including an African Union Executive Council, a Pan-African Parliament and an African Court of Justice," writes Corsi. According to him the future state is already officially designated by an emblem, a flag, an anthem, a central bank, and a unified continental military force.

The African Central Bank is supposed to create a continental currency. The present name of it during the phase of creation is "Gold Mandela." That shows the tendency of where this will lead to: Socialist power. Mandela is not a saint as dumb Westerners think, but as much a committed Communist as Vladimir Putin is.

On December 9, 2006, South American leaders of 12 nations agreed at a summit of the South American Community of Nations hosted by Bolivian President Evo Morales in Cochabamba, to create a high-level commission to study the idea of forming a continent wide community similar to the European Union. Among them were the Socialist/Communist government heads Luiz Inacio da Silva, Brazil, Hugo Chavez of Venezuela, Daniel Ortega of Nicaragua, Michelle Bachelet of Chile, Alan Garcia of Peru, Rafael Correa of Ecuador.

It becomes quite obvious that George W. Bush, pushing the project of a North American Community, is executing Soviet power policies, most likely without being aware of it. Block-building of nations leading to all nations being in one block (New World Order) was ad-opted by the Second Comintern (Communist International) Congress on July 28, 1920. "The aim of Socialism is not only to abolish the present division of mankind into small states, and all national isola-tion, not only brings the nations closer to each other, but also merge them…The merging of states is inevitable," stated Vladimir L Lenin, Communist leader and founder of the Soviet Union. His thinking has been expressed since then by quite a number of various Socialist and Conservative Western leaders.

We must not commit suicide giving up our sovereignty. Christians are the strongest block of voters in our nation and the voters now must speak up on the issue and fight for their sovereignty and freedom.

CHAPTER SIXTEEN

THE UNITED NATIONS HOAX

AMERICA AND THE West have not only lost the concept that history is meant to be a movement towards God but most of its leaders are actively engaged in dragging their nations in the opposite direction away from God without saying so. These nations have godless laws and procedures, and a pagan education system, in total, a godless infrastructure. The majority of their political and church leaders may have some religion but they and their nations don't have God. That means that something is fundamentally wrong with their leaders.

Hitler, as I described earlier, became chancellor on January 30, 1933, with 37 percent of the vote. He had never a majority. The conservatives had made arrangements with him which made him the head of the German government. They thought that Hitler in power would neutralize the Communist threat and that they would be able to control him.

They couldn't. Hitler had only used them for his own power purposes and it took just two months to put Germany on the road to totalitarianism. The conservatives had committed political suicide because they lacked a superior idea, absolute moral standards and therefore didn't recognize the reality of Hitler and the Nazis.

There are various political movements in the world of today which follow the same pattern. They seem to be of individual nature but are, in reality, part of the same bid for global power and aimed at disarming the main obstacle to that bid—American power. I see a repetition of Hitler's march to power leading us into a totalitarian society. Those who have put these movements into motion are lying about their real purposes like Hitler because those movements have only one purpose. And that is to fool conservative America and drag our nation into the totalitarian net headed by what is falsely labeled as the "United Nations." That label is meant to hide the real purpose of that international institution in the same way as Communist East Germany's label "wall of peace" for the Berlin Wall was meant to hide the ugly policy of holding the population prisoner of its unscrupulous regime.

Five major international political initiatives which are part of it have one thing in common—they lead to the strengthening of the potential global power of the godless United Nations and to the destruction of American sovereignty: her God-given mission of freedom and to the weakening of American power. In other words, this shift of power is the real reason for the initiatives and not the well-being of the American people or of humanity.

The United Nations began operations on October 24, 1945, with Soviet spy Alger Hiss as its first secretary general. If preventing future wars was a major reason for the creation of this institution then its performance has been a complete failure. According to the statistics provided by *American Minute of Bill Federer*, October 24, 2007, since its creation there have been over 100 million casualties in over 150 wars and armed conflicts around the globe.

The 185 members of the United Nations, however, spend $20 billion annually without ever being independently audited. There was also no attempt ever to condition the right of a member to vote in the General Assembly or the Security Council considering whether human rights as the UN proclaims them are being applied or not in the member state. *Outrage*, a recently published book by Dick Morris and Eileen

McGann, names 21 terror Sponsor states and Safe Havens with the right to vote. This, however, does not include Russia and China or the terrorist haven in Palestine nor the Middle East and other dictators.

Ten nations cover 75 percent of the UN budget, of which 49 percent comes from the United States with the highest annual contribution of $423 million, Japan $332 million and Germany $143 million, followed by the United Kingdom with $106 million, France with $103 million and Italy with $83 million, China pays $35 million and Russia less than the $20 million Switzerland pays.

The whole scheme is as absurd as is the institution itself, having for instance Japan pay $332 million and China a tenth of it apart from the fact that all these payments are a complete waste of money. The United Nations has nothing to contribute to the progress of humanity and is engaged in the destruction of free society. And who pays for all of it? The Western nations of course, which lifted humanity on a level of knowledge and wealth never achieved before and are now being manipulated into a totalitarian strait jacket, so that the class war minded members with their votes and our money can reach even deeper into Western pockets and distribute our wealth to the incompetent and corrupt bureaucrats around the world.

"The United Nations, created to be mankind's best hope for peace, has become the front for the largest corruption scandal in history: its Oil-for-Food Program," writes Dick Morris. $14 billion was stolen by UN employees, diplomats, member states, and two thousand companies through bribes, kick-backs, falsified accounting etc...The UN program director, Benon Sevan enriched himself with $150,000. France, Germany, Russia, and China had financial stakes in this scam operation and were opposed to the war in Iraq for that reason. The biggest winner in this operation was Saddam Hussein himself.

And this is only one of a multitude of scandals in which the United Nations has been involved in from time to time. This institution alone in its composition has neither character nor knowledge of justice to create and maintain peace. Why on earth do they exist and why on earth do we deal with them and waste our money with an institution which is not our friend and whose members are in the majority against us? We reject the truth of the matter and rather live in a dream world.

The Law of the Sea Treaty (LOST) is another attempt to cripple the United States, pick our pockets and empower the United Nations. If that law would become law, which Ronald Reagan refused to allow, the United Nations would be put into control of 70 percent of the world's surface. The LOST creates an entirely new government, complete with legislature, an executive, a judiciary, and a secretariat. This new government would have the authority to impose assessments and legal sanctions, as well as regulate air and sea commerce with the possibility that Americans could become subject to an international entity. There is also a provision that grants the new government the authority to tax American citizens and therewith enlarge their tax burden.

United States Senator Jeff Sessions who explained the matter to me commented: "The treaty also raises concerns for our security. Under the treaty, the United States could not board a foreign vessel even if it is suspected of carrying weapons of mass destruction. This proposal undermines President Bush's Proliferation Security Initiative and would make our nation more vulnerable to a terrorist attack."

"I refuse to support any treaty that raises taxes for American citizens, diminishes the authority of our Constitution and threatens our security. The LOST is unnecessary, and in light of recent UN scandals, it would be unwise to grant new authority or additional funding to the U.N, or its progeny."

Global Warming is another attempt to put the United Nations into the center of a global movement. I cannot go into the details of the proposition in the framework of this book since I am not a scientist. The issue is whether man is responsible for climate changes or not.

The UN with Al Gore in the forefront assert that that is so and to the delight of the industries involved in climate related business created an expensive plan to address the problem. There is, however, enough material from prestigious scientists who take issue with their conclusions and reason that that is not so. According to a U.S. Senate report at the end of 2007 hundreds of prominent scientists state that global warming cannot be attributed to man's activities.

During an interview by Glen Back in the CNN-Television channel *Headline News,* the president of the Weather Channel, John Coleman, stated that *Global Warming* is the biggest scam ever, built on lies and disregarding thousands of scientists who signed a disclaimer of the fraud. As an example he pointed out that NBC is one of the strongest promoters of the Global Warming fairy tale. However NBC is owned by General Electric which is heavily invested in environmental business.

Earlier in this book, I demonstrated how the North American Union project would lead straight into a totalitarian system.

Under no circumstances should the United States cede control of the internet to the United Nations. It would be used immediately to get us on the road to global mind control and silence those who want to use the freedom of speech. Amendments 1 and 2 would disappear as have already the intentions of our founding fathers about the substance of freedom.

CHAPTER SEVENTEEN

SYSTEMS OF LIES

I SHALL NOW look at relativism from the angle of the lie, which is presented as truth, as a consequence producing moral aberrations, and becoming the basis of a dictatorship of relativism. Some of the aberrations I pointed out earlier but to go deeper, I am going to expand on a chapter appearing in my previous book, *Moral Meltdown the Core of Globalism* titled "The Lie."

In August of 1966 a study at the University of Virginia concluded that everyone lies at least once a day. According to a report by the Washington Times of January 28, 2008 a survey by a British beverage firm found that each American will tell 88,000 lies during a life time. That means 4 lies per day. Lying has become normal behavior. Harvard philosopher Sissela Bok pointed out that almost all lies are damaging. My own lying brought me closer to the Nazis and further from God. I made a decision never to lie again and I am convinced that lies are at the root of all our problems. We live in a fog of lies, which grows thicker every day and makes us unable to see reality.

The German philosopher Karl Jaspers defines lies as follows: "One may lie by language by deliberately asserting something which is false. It means lying to others but not to oneself, one is misusing the language. But a further step is also possible. By lying the lie may reach a stage in which a person finally believes his own lies so that the distinction between truth and falsehood is lost…Untruth may range from the shameless lie which is immediately recognizable to a total inextricable system of lies which is put forward with the conviction of an actor who no longer perceives himself as an actor. The individual is then trapped in his own world of lies. Words have lost their consistent sense. Sometimes they are understood as the interlocutor understands them and then they are taken to mean the opposite." Thus lies are elevated into principle. As Jaspers put it, "Truth and fiction are combined in such a way that nothing good arises, but the radical lie itself becomes reality."

Lawrence Dawson speaks in his book, "The Death of Reality" of the "systematic denial of reality." "The very idea of reality has become 'untenable' in our current society," he writes. "People have begun to live in pink-clouds and fantasies, a state which they neither recognize nor can associate with any reason or cause."

We are lying to each other and we are being lied to by our government establishment day-in, day-out. We are given reasons which sound good but do not represent the real motivation of the politician who offers them. We are being manipulated in exactly the same way as the German people were manipulated by the Nazis. I started this book explaining how Hitler began World War II with the lie that Germany was attacked by Polish army units. Practically all major political shifts to his totalitarian rule happened before the war because of the lies he used to deceive the German people. He also lied to heads of foreign governments about his intentions.

His lies caused millions of people to die. Lying for power, however, was and is not limited to Hitler. One can nearly say it has become the rule in Western democracies, and that lying has made genuine consensus between different political groupings very difficult and very often impossible. I also pointed out that the "smallest" lie of "little me" helped Hitler's lies, that no lie is without consequences, and that every lie harms somebody.

Slander and lies and the rewriting of history on that basis for political reasons have become reality in the minds of millions of people and of whole nations. A great part of humanity lives in a dream world which does not exist and acts accordingly. Individual lies form a system of lies when taken as a whole and can dominate a given society. Once a specific lie is institutionalized and becomes a basis for policy decisions, for legislation and law enforcement, then it advances the formation of a system of lies. The more lies that are being elevated this way, the closer we get to a system where lies dominate. If this continues, the next and final phase leads to a society where lies rule, or in other words, to godless and totalitarian rule. Nazi and Communist societies, both Socialist, were and are such societies. Lies are being enforced with the power of government and opposing the lie is being treated as a criminal act.

There is no free speech and no right to bear arms. Totalitarian societies are the result of lies and not of economic deprivation. The liar however, and that title includes just about everybody, is concerned with him- or herself and does not notice the gradual transformation of the society he or she lives in from freedom to slavery. He or she doesn't do anything to reverse the trend except perhaps criticizing the other political party.

Many lies are installed as laws in America and we are already partly covered by a shroud of lies. It will inevitably lead to the loss of freedom and a totalitarian system of lies unless the little liar changes, stops lying, and stands up for truth. I am a prime example for the fact that people can change from moral defeat to a clean life and make a difference. That moral change and a change of direction on all levels of human society are possible is the only hope for humanity. And forget the nonsense of the United Nations.

To the Christian: in St. John, 8: 44–45 Jesus defines before a Jewish audience eager to kill him the founder and father of the lie. "Every man who commits sin is a slave…Why can't you understand what I am saying? It is because you are unable to do so. For you are the children of your father the Devil and you love to do the evil things you do. He was a murderer from the beginning and always hated the truth. There is no truth in him. When he lies it is consistent with his character, for he is a liar and the father of lies. So when I tell the truth, you just naturally do not believe me."

He did not make a distinction between big and small lies because any lie is an insult to God; any lie enslaves those who utter them. And who defines what a big or small lie is? There is a saying that huge doors swing in small hinges, and that means that breaking the hinge can bring the door down.

CHAPTER EIGHTEEN

THE ROLE OF GOD IN HUMAN SOCIETY

THE DICTATORSHIP OF RELATIVISM

POPE BENEDICT XVI hit the nail on the head when he spoke of the Dictatorship of Relativism. This dictatorship must be broken. That definition is relevant to all societies on earth, including ours today. Relativism is the problem, which, however, needs to be exactly defined. Godlessness and relativism are the same because it means rejection of God by rejecting His absolute moral standards. The acceptance of moral absolutes by individuals and society is the only viable alternative to self-destruction. It is the only way to free mankind from this dictatorship; no political manipulation can do it.

There are many wars being fought in the world today but the real existential war is the ideological war about the role of God in global society. For us, the pressing priority is to restore God into the center of American life and politics. God created this nation with a mission: freedom. And lasting freedom is only possible with truth. Without God at the heart of American government there will be no freedom in the world. Christians can't allow liars, unrepentant adulterers, perjurers, ignorant of reality to lead America. As I learned through the Nazi catastrophe it is character which comes first and not issues, character decides about the way issues are being handled.

In Nazi society every single section of it was corrupted and subjugated to Nazi purposes: religion, the judicial system, education, sports, etc…Civil government was engaged in doing the opposite of what it was intended for: protecting its citizens. By law, Jews were stripped of their rights and citizenship, and those who tried to help them, were punished and normally executed. Soviet society has different labels but the same principle of relativism and communist prerogatives in every section of their society. Both are and were dictatorships of relativism. There is no way a free society can merge with a totalitarian socialist system, the goal which Mr. Gorbachev promotes. The attempt to do so would mean for us to first abandon truth and then liberty. A politician who teams up with Gorbachev is an enemy of the American nation.

THE CONFUSION OF CHRISTIANS

When I drove friends of ours, a couple, to the airport in Miami one day we had a discussion about religion. I said something along the lines that the only sane road for America and humanity to take is to obey God's Commandments. She objected and said that not everybody believed in the Christian religion and that we couldn't force our views on them. I answered that the issue was not religion and that it didn't make any difference whether somebody believed in God or not because God's Commandments are obligatory for every last person on earth regardless of what their religion is and whether they believe in God or not. She was horrified about my "self-righteous intolerance" and asked: "Do you think that we Christians are better than all the others and that our religion is right and the other religions are wrong?"

I answered that this was not a question of being better than others or others being inferior, but about truth and how humanity can live together as equals instead of fighting and killing each other. I confirmed to her, however, that other religions were definitely wrong, and if she didn't think so, then she would not be a Christian as she claimed to be. If God is merely the religious expression of what some people believe, then you could discuss with others whether something else might also be right or even better. And that is the position into which the enemies of God and freedom have maneuvered our politicians and Christians.

But God is reality. He created the universe and all mankind, and laid down the rules to live by for everybody regardless what their background is and what they believe in. His Commandments must be put into place in all nations beginning with ours. If we put our house in order, other nations will follow our example.

To stand on that ground and not waiver has nothing to do with intolerance. It is the reason for the existence of the United States of America, and it is the basis for our federal Constitution and the Constitutions of all fifty states of the Union. To quote only one, the Preamble of Alabama Constitution states: "We the people of the state of Alabama, invoking the favor and guidance of Almighty God, do ordain and establish the following Constitution." The Declaration of Independence states: "We hold these Truths to be self-evident, that all Men are created equal, that they are endowed by their Creator with certain unalienable Rights, that among those are Life, Liberty, and the Pursuit of Happiness—that to secure these Rights, Governments are instituted among men…" Is our government doing it? If I look at the three branches of government it doesn't look like it to me.

We celebrate the Day of Independence, but in our schools they teach Darwin's theory of evolution. The substance of the Declaration of Independence and Darwin's theory exclude each other. Darwinism apart from being wrong is unconstitutional because it denies our inalienable rights given by God on which our Constitution and our nation are built. The government establishment, however, does not "secure these rights" but instead, allows them to be taken from us. They will have to account for this when they meet their creator. They should face the parents and the pastors if these would only fight for the souls of their children.

In his essay "Does Darwinism Devalue Human life?" Richard Weikart, Professor of History at the California State University points out that Darwin in his Autobiography rejects the idea of objective moral standards, stating that one "can have for his rule of life, as far as I can see, only to follow those impulses and instincts which are the strongest or which seem to him to be the best ones." Friedrich Hellward, an influential ethnologist, Weikart writes, promoted a Darwinian view of social evolution in his major work *The History of Culture (18750)*. Hellward is of the opinion that the struggle for existence is above all moral considerations. "The right of the stronger," Weikart writes, "is a natural law."

You can take out the name Friedrich Hellward and put in instead Adolf Hitler and it would be correct. That was his theme in explaining his aggressive plans and actions. That was the theme we were told in school and in the Hitler Youth constantly, as I reported earlier in this book. Darwin's theory helped the Nazis to destroy morality and lead the nation into self destruction. The same thing is happening here now. The youth under totalitarian Nazi rule and the American youth in our "free" country are being fed the same poison of relativism only with different labels, by people with the same or similar purpose. That is not what our Founding Fathers fought, sacrificed and died for. It must be changed.

Of the 56 signers of the Declaration of Independence, 17 lost their fortunes, 12 had their homes destroyed, 5 became prisoners of war, 1 had two sons imprisoned on the British starving ship Jersey, 1 had a son killed in battle, 1 had his wife die from harsh prison treatment and 9 signers died during the War.

John Hancock signed first, saying "The price on my head has just doubled." Benjamin Franklin added, "We must hang together or most assuredly we hang separately."

Equally to the point were Samuel Adams' words "We have this day restored the Sovereign to whom all men ought to be obedient. He reigns in Heaven and from the rising to the setting of the sun, let His kingdom come." When we celebrate our Independence Day let us take to heart what John Adams said, "I am apt to believe that it will be celebrated by succeeding generations as the great anniversary Festival. It ought to be commemorated, as the Day of Deliverance, by solemn acts of devotion to God Almighty."

Chief Justice John Marshall, 4th Chief Justice of the Supreme Court wrote to Jasper Adams on May 9, 1833: "The American population is entirely Christian, and with us Christianity and Religion are identified. It would be strange indeed, if with such a people, our institutions did not presuppose Christianity and did not often refer to it and exhibit with it."

How many politicians have I heard saying that they are Christians but cannot force their religious views on others, and therefore have to keep their religious views out of the political process? This of course is suicidal nonsense, and every American needs to be clear about it. The issue is not the religious views of a politician but God's moral absolutes in government and whether he or she lives by them. The real issue is the reality of God's moral absolutes in the life of a politician, because there is a correlation between the politician's relation to those moral absolutes and the political decisions he or she makes.

Very uncomfortable, isn't it? If you keep God from the political process, you invite disaster—as it happened in Germany, the godless ran the German nation into the ground and they are at it again. America is no different! All Christians need to constantly look at the voting record of their representatives because it will show what really guides them.

It is also a misconception to think that trying to persuade somebody else means to force one's religious views on others. I think that the shadow of the Middle Ages, when the kings forced their subjects to specific rules of worship, still looms over America. People are afraid that some fanatic might force everybody into a set of rules. Primitive people adhering to formal requirements like the Taliban and their brothers-in-arms or those who promote political correctness, which in Germany under Hitler was called "the party line," only prove that they do not have a relevant message and must therefore resort to lies and force in order to prevail. True religion promotes love and not hatred. I am talking about convincing others by example, through the life you live and the society you create. And if I look at the American society of today, I have to say that it doesn't look very convincing.

The American scene gives a contradictory picture. I believe that America is still a bulwark of freedom because there is a solid Christian and moral substance in certain sections of society. But it is also true that America's Christian heritage is being attacked mercilessly and constantly. The moral battles being fought show that Christians and Conservatives are leading a defensive campaign and the majority does not fight. There is no unity of purpose and action.

The reason for that is small thinking and moral compromises. I live with the knowledge that Germany, in spite of martyrs like Dietrich Bonhoeffer and Claus von Stauffenberg, went down the drain because millions of church-goers gave evil leaders a free hand. A majority of pastors who do not comply with their job namely fight that government leaders act according to God's Commandments. Not only are the terrorists evil, but all those who defy God's Commandments in the way he or she lives and acts are as well. The defensive posture of American Conservatives and Christians can have no other reason and it is urgent to find the offensive edge.

They have to recognize that the insurrection against God that started centuries ago is picking up speed. It is meant to destroy the power of God and establish the rule of almighty man. The battle is for power, and morality is the battle ground. The insurrection against God means the organized abandonment of His moral order and replacing it with a global social and political infrastructure contrary to His Commandments yet capable of integrating toothless Christian religion. This is possible because comfortable Christians have reduced the Christian revolution meant to transform the world to a meek message of personal salvation. As a consequence, we are leaving absolute moral standards behind.

The movement to godlessness is in full swing but most "Christians" do not understand what is happening and neither do the politicians. The mentality of irrelevance was best expressed by a statement of all protestant bishops—except one—in East Germany to the Communist government. It defined the Christian task as "demonstrating how to live as Christians in a Socialist society." Utterly ridiculous! They should have stood up as a body and attacked the lies of the atheist rulers of their flock. But instead they did the same thing church leaders did in Nazi Germany during the persecution of the Jews: they kept their silence. They might have followed the path of Jesus, Peter, Paul, and thousands of others.

Thomas Merton pointed out that a person "who has meditated on the Passion of Christ but has not meditated on the extermination camps of Dachau and Auschwitz has not yet fully entered into the experience of Christianity in our time." Richard J. Foster comments that this kind of meditation is best accomplished with the Bible in one hand and the newspaper in the other.

I know the reality that personal and national sins cannot be separated because I lived it and it is not a personal view. The multicultural concept is the consequence of the wrongful separation of God and society. It ignores the reality of human nature and nationhood, tramples on the traditions which are different in every country as well as on national purpose and character, and leads to the destruction of Western civilization.

It explains why George W. Bush ignores the wishes of the majority of the American people with regards to the issue of illegal aliens and the formation of the North American Union Collective. He has experienced a Christian rebirth but his Christian concepts and consequently his policies remain insufficient. But he can change like everybody else, and change he must. And if he does he will find that moral change in people is the only viable alternative to organizing people and nations into a godless government structures against the will of his voters.

WE THE PEOPLE WANT:

—A president, whose family life is an example for everybody.

—A person who is connected with the American history and advances the nation's mission.

—Somebody who doesn't lie and knows how to define freedom as moral criteria and not just as an economic and political necessity.

—Who is committed to truth as a person and as a responsible leader of the United States defends it in our laws and social infrastructure.

—Somebody who opens the doors of our schools and government institutions to God.

—Who fights to end the shedding of children's blood in the name of the "Right to Choose."

—A man or a woman who makes God central again in our national affairs and defends our sovereignty.

—And a man who insists upon education in our schools that teaches the courage of our founding fathers and makes our Constitution central.

THE LOST PURPOSE OF HISTORY

Christian teachings include the concept that mankind's history is a moving process which culminates in the second coming of Christ and the establishment of the Kingdom of God on earth. Eschatology is the doctrine concerning the "last things"—the final consummation of God's purposes in creation and the final destination of individual souls and all of humanity. All of humanity means what it says, all humanity whatever race, religion or nationality a nation or a person may have.

This Christian concept was stolen by the fabricators of materialistic ideologies who replaced the divine link to eternity with a secular culmination in their hate-driven ideologies. The National Socialists, Socialists generally called Nazis, had a vision of a German national community and a world run by the master race—they themselves. The final destination for international Socialists, the Communist Marxists/Leninists, was defined as a global Socialist and classless society which, however, would be a totalitarian system run by godless functionaries. The destination of radical Islam is a Muslim world where the Muftis rule and no other religion exists. Those who kill "unbelievers" who refuse to convert to Islam are promised rewards in paradise.

Followers of these three godless ideologies consider themselves part of a process in which they change the direction of history to reach their final destination. They are groomed to invest their whole existence and life into achieving victory for their ideology. This is also a perversion of the Christian teaching that Almighty God wants the whole person and not just some part.

The West has lost the concept that history is meant to be a movement of humanity toward God. It has eliminated Christian teachings as irrelevant for the political process and has reduced the Christian message to a purely personal affair. Western Christians love their comfort and do not want to risk their quality of life. Western nations and their political and religious leaders therefore do not understand the purpose and motives of their ideological enemies, nor do they understand their mindset. They have their own mindset and mistakenly assume that others think as they do. They are addressing the symptoms individually but not the global substance. That is why we remain in the defense, are being manipulated, are losing the ideological war and will never win unless we change.

America and the Western world have to go back to their roots in order to understand the nature of our organized enemies, and to defeat them. They have also to understand the difference between the substance of a religion and the manner how this substance is being promoted.

Revolution of Truth and Freedom

Political and religious leaders have to do some thinking and come up with a message, which is not religious or partisan, but universal. It must be a message of truth, a message that applies to everybody on this planet; that links the individual to his or her nation and to humanity, to life on earth, and eternity. We need a message so that persons who want to see a better world can apply it, fight for it, do it not just on Sundays, but every day, all the time, with all their lives and fortunes. I believe truth is the key issue for everyone. Since freedom is the mission of the American nation and its people, and since freedom without truth cannot last, the battle for truth must be at the heart of the battle for America.

However, we must realize that political freedom is only part of the substance of freedom as important as it is. Alexander Solzhenitsyn pointed out: "The most important part of our freedom, inner freedom, is always subject to our will. If we surrender to corruption, we do not deserve to be called human. But let us note that the absolutely essential task is not political liberation, but the liberation of our souls from participation in the lie forced upon us, then it requires no physical, revolutionary, social organizational measures, no meetings, strikes, trade unions. No. It requires from each individual a moral step within his or her power—no more than that. No one who voluntarily runs with hounds of falsehood will ever be able to justify himself to the living, or to posterity, or to his friends, or to his children." He referred to Soviet society—in the meanwhile it is also relevant to democratic society.

Truth is only truth if it is absolute. Absolute truth is God's truth, and it is the same for all. To fight for truth means to define and attack the lie. To destroy the power of the lie means to destroy the dictatorship of relativism and begin to build the kingdom of God on earth. You begin with yourself and not with others but by casting the lie from your own life. I explained how I did it. Attacking the lie and standing up for truth means turning godlessness into God-guided faith.

In his speech "The Sin of Silence" to the students of the Baptist Midwestern Seminary in Kansas City on September 6, 2000, Pastor Wilson said:

To compare what is happening in America today to Nazi Germany is no mere flight of rhetorical exaggeration. This nation is heedlessly stumbling toward millennium darkness. Look around you and read the signs of the times. Look beyond the walls of our beautiful sanctuaries and the comfort of our padded pews to see the chaos, the corruption and the confusion, that reigns throughout our culture. We live in a society where passions are riderless horses, uncontrolled and uncontrollable, in which there is a desolation of decency, in which love has become a jungle emotion, lust exalted to lordship, sin elevated to sovereignty, Satan adored as, and man magnified above his maker.

The great reformer Martin Luther once declared 'that the preacher who does not rebuke the sins of the rulers through God's word spoken publicly, boldly, and honestly, strengthens the sins of the tyrants, and becomes a partaker in them and bears responsibility for them.'

In the face of monstrous evil, he who keeps silent fails in his responsibility before God and shares in his guilt. The moral meltdown that has overtaken America has been met with a deafening silence from the pulpits of America and the people-pleasing preachers who presume to stand in them. This desolation of decency could not have occurred if the pulpits of this land were once again aflame with righteousness, to use Alexis de Tocqueville's famous words. By our apathy, by our acquiescence and by our ignorance, the church of Jesus Christ has consigned itself to irrelevance and impotence in the ongoing struggle for the soul of America.

In 1940, at the height of Hitler's power and popularity, a courageous young pastor named Dietrich Bonhoeffer denounced the church's failure to speak out against the evil. In 1940 that lonely voice of truth proclaimed, 'we in the church must confess that we have not proclaimed often or clearly enough the message of the one God, who has revealed himself for all time in Christ Jesus and who will tolerate no other Gods besides Himself. She must confess her timidity, her cowardice, her evasiveness and her dangerous concessions. She was silent when she should have cried out, because of the blood of the innocent was crying aloud to heaven. The Church must confess the lawless application of brutal force, the physical and spiritual suffering of countless innocent people, oppression, hatred, and murder, and that she has not raised her voice on behalf of the victims and has not found ways to hasten to their aid. The Church is guilty of the deaths of the weakest and most defenseless brothers of Jesus Christ. The Church must confess that she has desired security and peace, quiet, possessions and honor, to which she has no right. She has not borne witness to the truth of God. And by her silence, she has rendered herself guilty because of her unwillingness to suffer for what she knows to be right.

God is a factor in America. The French and most Europeans do not understand that America is different from them, that we are not like any other democracy because we have a different moral basis and a national purpose beyond self. They try to have America accept authorization of the United Nations for possible actions to defend ourselves. That of course would be unconstitutional and furthermore very dumb. The majority of the members either have no clue whatsoever about what is needed to defend this nation, do not know freedom, or are our enemies.

What do those who sit in the Security Council know about freedom? Do they know that freedom without truth cannot last? Do they even attempt to be truthful? Do the nations which send their representatives to New York respect the rights of the common people in their own countries? Are Americans with the finest God-centered Constitution on earth supposed to listen to corrupt pagans? There are at least three godless states among the five permanent members with veto power: Russia, China, and France.

It is interesting to note that the former "conservative" French President Jacques Valerie d'Estaing joined then "conservative" President Jacques Chirac and Socialists like the then German Chancellor Gerhard Schroeder in efforts to prevent any reference to God in the European Constitution. What those three men have in common is godlessness. Godlessness was the principal reason for the crimes of the Nazi leaders. Contrary to the American Revolution, which was a revolution of Christians who strived for political and religious freedom, the French Revolution was part of the insurrection of Humanity against God.

It is because of godlessness that the European leaders are unable to see in political developments the unfolding of history and the substance of what is happening. If you take God out of the equation, then you are as blind as a bat. That is true in the position of any nation toward Israel and the Middle East which fail to take God's guiding of Israel, His promises and the biblical substance into consideration.

Watching the formation of the anti-God alliance I believe that we have to find a way to unite the God obeying forces for meaningful ideological action. Nothing in this world will last if it is not anchored in truth. The principle of truth is the same for all men and nations regardless of color, race, class or religion. Everybody and every nation are expected and have the capacity to live in truth. Humanity's critical challenge of the hour is that of reconciling our innermost motives—those of each individual human being—with the charge and mission with which God has endowed our human natures. In that way, His great creation, God's plan for humanity may unfold. It is God's divine plan that then will guide our activities, regulate our social existence and afford solutions to all our problems, whether we encounter them in our personal life or in society as a whole.

This linking of our innermost motives with the truth of God is especially required in the hearts of the leaders of our nations, and principally in the hearts of the leaders of America. Then a nation under God can become a reality, which can lead the world to freedom. To make truth the basis of all human relationships is the task of this 21st century. Truth must be the battle cry for the second American Revolution.

THE NATIONAL INSTITUTE FOR TRUTH AND FREEDOM

OBJECTIVES

THE OBJECTIVES OF the National Institute for Truth and Freedom, founded by Hilmar von Campe, are to make the battle for freedom the concern of every last person in the United States and across the world. Freedom for the American people can only last if Americans honor their Constitution and Godly heritage. Otherwise the godless will chip away one bit of freedom after the other. Freedom is the mission, given by God to America at her birth as a nation. It means to change the world. For more information log on to: www.voncampe.com.

Freedom is only possible on the basis of truth and the 20th Century clarified the sobering reality that lies destroy freedom. Materialistic ideologies and government systems based on lies robbed hundreds of millions of people of their freedom and millions of their life. The battle for freedom therefore is the battle for truth by breaking the power of the lie, and trying to establish truth as the basis of all human relationships. Truth must begin reigning in the heart of every human being, beginning with every American.

A practical part in breaking the power of the lie, for instance, is to help the Europeans understand American purposes and mentality, and counter the global smear campaign against this country. By the same token part of it is also to make Americans understand the nature of the lies at the heart of Nazi, Marxist, and Islamic philosophies and their implications for our society of today.

The institute will strive together with all patriots to make a nation under God a reality, which through her people and government gives moral leadership to a world that hungers for selfless and inspired leaders. We want to add strength to the growing movement for freedom in the world, and to the fight and sacrifice of a myriad of people in the United States for that purpose in the face of growing violence and hatred about everywhere. The institute is dedicated to the reconciliation of people and nations and promotes the rule of law across the globe. It also wants to help eliminate misunderstandings and divisions between nations which should be united by a common purpose.

The institute is to give a legal framework to the above activities and to receive donations to achieve the stated objectives. This is to be done through promotion of books, articles, keynote addresses, radio interviews, and television appearances. Additionally, we will strive to reach our objectives through the support of education and public discussion on the nature of freedom and how to make it permanent, as well as conferences and any other means we may deem appropriate.

We will also pursue educational programs regarding the central role of the American Constitution as an outstanding political instrument in the belief that it remains the best example for the constitutions of many if not all other countries. It will be shown that the sanctity of human life and sound, whole families are indispensable conditions for a free society. Donations, not yet deductible, can be sent to account no. 242 0494 4 at Compass Bank, 920 Fairhope Ave., AL 36532 (or at any Compass Bank in Florida, Alabama, Texas, Arkansas, New Mexico and Colorado) or per mail to P.O. Box 1746, Fairhope, AL 36532-2116.

Founder and President

Hilmar von Campe

THE INTERNATIONAL BIOGRAPHICAL CENTER IN CAMBRIDGE, ENGLAND,

THE INTERNATIONAL WHO'S WHO OF INTELLECTUALS, 1992

HILMAR VON CAMPE is particularly interested in development towards a global society and ethics. His book, *Cowardice and Appeasement* is not an isolated endeavor at a late stage of life, but the integrated part of a lifetime study and commitment in which even twenty years of business activities are subordinated to the overriding purposes as he describes then in his book. Hilmar von Campe was, in the fifties, in the forefront of building the human relationships between people of different European countries who fought each other over generations, out of which we see now the emergence of a new and free Europe. In the sixties he lived and traveled through most of the Latin American continent, lived in the homes of ordinary people and argued with Presidents, Generals, Priests and Students and learned to understand their different ways of thinking and acting. Finally in the seventies and eighties he was at the heart of the issues that dominate the relations between the industrialized and developing nations. As a member of the American Chamber of Commerce of Mexico he was for many years chairman of its subcommittee on foreign investments. He was helped in his understanding of the issues by his university degree in economics, as economics not liberated not liberal arts are at the heart of the emerging new world's order. His domination of languages—he is fluent in German, English,

Spanish and understands some French—have helped him to firsthand experiences and in the in-depth research of social economic in so many parts of the world. Hilmar von Campe is truly a professional who has followed over decades in different activities, the same purpose of investigating the underlying forces in our and other societies, to show how to change distortions and injustices and to help humanity into growing into a global society of equals...Until 1971 he was in banking, and 1971–73 Assistant to the President and Secretary of the Board of Management of ADELA Investment Company, South America, and then Regional Manager of the Caribbean area with them until 1976. He was then Financial Counselor IHM Ltd. St. Lucia and Manager of Cotinco SA. in Mexico. Since 1979 he has run a small automotive part company, since 1986 additionally a travel agency and since 1989 has been an author dedicated to the freedom and dignity of men.

THE WEIZMANN-FAISAL AGREEMENT

JANUARY 1919

HIS ROYAL HIGHNESS the Emir FAISAL, representing and acting on behalf of the Arab Kingdom of HEJAZ, and Dr. Ciam Weizmann, representing and acting on behalf of the Zionist Organization, mindful of the racial kinship and ancient bonds existing between the Arabs and the Jewish people, and realizing that the surest means of working out the consummation of their nation aspirations, is through the closest possible collaboration in the development of the Arab State and Palestine, and being desirous further of confirming the good understanding which exists between them, have agreed upon the following articles:

Article I

The Arab State and Palestine in their relations and undertakings shall be controlled by the most cordial goodwill and understanding and to this end Arab and Jewish duly accredited agents shall be established and maintained in their respective territories.

Article II

Immediately following the completion of deliberations of the Peace Conference, the definite boundaries between the Arab State and Palestine shall be determined by a commission to be agreed upon by the parties hereto.

Article III

In the establishment of the Constitution and Administration of Palestine all such measures shall be adopted as will afford the fullest guarantees for carrying into effect the British Government's Declaration of the 2nd of November 1917 (Balfour Declaration).

Article IV

All necessary measures will be taken to encourage and stimulate the immigration of Jews into Palestine on a large scale, and as quickly as possible to settle Jewish upon the land through closer settlement and intensive cultivation of the soil. In taking such measures the Arab peasants and tenant farmers shall be protected in their rights, and shall be assisted in forwarding their economic development.

Article V

No regulation or law shall be made prohibiting or interfering in any way with the free exercise of religion; and further the free exercise and expression of religious profession and worship without discrimination or preference shall forever be allowed. No religious test shall ever be required for the exercise of civil or religious rights.

Article VI

The Mohammedan Holy Places shall be under Mohammedan control.

Article VII

The Zionist Organization proposes to send to Palestine a commission of experts to make a survey of the economic possibilities of the country, and to report upon the best means for its development. The Zionist Organization will use its best efforts to assist the Arab in providing the means for developing the natural resources and economic possibilities thereof.

Article VIII

The parties hereto agree to act in complete accord and harmony in all matters embraced herein before the Peace Conference.

Article IX

Any matters of dispute, which may arise between the contracting parties, shall be referred to the British Government for arbitration.

Given under our hand at London, England, the Third Day of January, One Thousand Nine Hundred and Nineteen.

Provided the Arabs obtain their independents as demanded in my memorandum dated 4th of January, 1919, to the Foreign Office of the Government of Great Britain, I shall concur in the above articles. But if the slightest departure or modification were to be made I shall not then be bound by a single word of the present Agreement which shall be deemed void and of no account or validity, and I shall not be answerable in any way whatsoever.

Faisal Ibn Hussein

Chaim Weizmann

BIBLIOGRAPHY

Boff, Leonardo und Clodovis, *Wie betreibt man Theologie der Befreiung,* (*How to Practice Theology of Liberation*), Parmos, Duesseldorf 1980

Bukovski Vladimir and Stroilov Pavel, EUSSR, *Die Sowjetischen Wurzeln der Europaeischen Integration,* (*The Soviet Roots of the European Integration*), Claus Peter Clausen Verlag, Lippstadt 1996

Brock, David, *The Seduction of Hillary Rodham,* The Free Press, New York 1996

von Campe, Hilmar, *Feigheit und Anpassung,* (*Cowardice and Appeasement*),Universitas Verlag, Muenchen 1989

Cohen, Ben, *Israel, Arabs and the Middle East,* Har Tavor Publishing, Wynnewood 1992

Foster, Richard J., *Celebration of Discipline,* Harper, San Francisco 1998

Friedrich, Jörg, *Der Brand,* (*The Fire*), Propyläen Verlag, Munic 2002

Gutierrez, Gustavo, *Theologia de la Liberacion, Perspectivas,* Ediciones Sigueme, Salamanca 1985

Hancock, Graham, *The Lords of Poverty,* The Atlantic Monthly Press, New York 1989

Hoffmann, Joachim, *Stalin's War of Extermination, 1941–1945, Planning, Realization and Documentation,* Theses & Dissertations Press, Capshaw 2001

Liang, Qiao and Xiangsui, Wang, *Unrestricted Warfare,* Pan American Publishing, Panama City 2002

Malik, S. K., *The Quranic Concept of War,* Himalayan Books, New Delhi 1986

Monteith, Stanley, *Brotherhood of Darkness,* Hearthstone Publishing, Oklahoma City 2000

Morris, Dick and Eileen McGann, *Outrage,* Harper Collins Publishers, New York 2007

Morse, Chuck, *The Nazi Connection to Islamic Terrorism—Adolf Hitler and Haj Amin al-Husseini*, Universe New York, Lincoln Shanghai 2003

Nawratil, Heinz, *Verteibungsverbrechen an Deutschen, (Crimes Expulsing Germans from Their Homes)*, Universitas, Munic 1982

Pacepa, Ion Mihai, *Red Horizons, Chronicles of a Communist Spy Chief*, Regnery Gateway, Washington DC, 1987

Sears, Alan and Osten Craig, *The ACLU vs. America*, Broadman & Holman Publishers, Nashville Tennessee 2005

Smith, Ian D., *The Great Betrayal*, Blake Publishers, Gardena 1997

Spieß Alfred and Lichtenstein Heiner, *Unternehmen Tannenberg*, (*Enterprise Tannenberg*), Limes Verlag, Wiesbaden and Munic 1979

Story, Christopher, *The European Union Collective—Enemy of Its Member States*, Edward Hale Ltd., London and New York 2001

Suvurov, Victor, *Der Eisbrecher* (*The Icebraker*), Klett-Cotta, Stuttgart 1989

Strauss, Wolfgang, *Projekt Barbarossa*, Herbig, Munic 1998

Topitsch, Ernst, *Stalin's Krieg (Stalin's War)*, Busse-Seewald, Herford 1990

Intelligence Reports, Newspapers and Magazines

Communist Manifest
Die Welt, Germany
Financial Intelligenz Report, Newsmax
Front Page Magazine
Guysen Israel News
Howard Phillips, Issues and Strategic Bulletin
Human Events
Jewish Virtual Connections
National Review Online
Wall Street Journal
Washington Times
WorldNetDaily

ABOUT THE AUTHOR

HILMAR VON CAMPE was born on April 11, 1925, in Germany. He was in the Hitler Youth and is a WWII Veteran. He has an economics degree from the University of Hamburg and went to Latin America where he spent a great part of his adult life in various countries like Argentina, Brasil, Peru and Mexico. For 18 years he was a fulltime volunteer for the global ideological movement *Moral Rearmament,* trying to change the world. In 1971 he changed into a financial job, and he worked for the international investment company ADELA, which had its headquarters in Lima, Peru, where he married Dina Gamio. From Peru he went to Jamaica and managed the Caribbean area for Adela.

From there he went to Mexico City, where he was first managing a consulting company for foreign investors and then made himself independent as managing director of an automotive parts factory. He also owned a travel agency. For many years he was chairman of the subcommittee on foreign investments of The American Chamber of Commerce.

In 1990 he came to the United States. At an age where other people retire, he started a new business as a legal immigrant and wrote six books. He founded the National Institute for Truth and Freedom. In 2004 he became an American citizen.

Hilmar von Campe is listed in the 1992 *International Who's Who of Intellectuals* of the International Biographical Center in Cambridge, England. Having grown up under the Nazis, he offers a unique perspective on the rise and fall of Nazi Germany. He says that there are many similarities between the Nazi society and America of today. Fighting for a change of direction of his nation of choice, he is proud to be an American citizen. His son Stefan is about to get married, and his daughter Sabrina is married to Marcelo Lew. They have a daughter Sophie.